Wolves in my Head

By Davy E.

Within each of us there is a good wolf & a bad wolf

They forever battle to control our minds

Which one will win the battle?

The Autobiography of a Recovering Alcoholic.

Includes the poems

"The Grateful Alcoholic" & "The Battle of the Wolves"

1

Contents

Wolves in my Head

Dedication

Dedicated in gratitude to my Wife & Children in the hope that they may gain some understanding of the disease I suffer from, and what makes me tick. They stood by me when I didn't deserve them, and loved me even when I was cold hearted. Such is the nature of unconditional love.

Acknowledgements

The Twelve Steps are reprinted with permission of Alcoholics Anonymous World Services, Inc. ("AAWS") Permission to reprint the Twelve Steps does not mean that AAWS has reviewed or approved the contents of this publication, or that AAWS necessarily agrees with the views expressed herein. A.A. is a program of recovery from alcoholism only - use of the Twelve Steps in connection with programs and activities which are patterned after A.A., but which address other problems, or in any other non-A.A. context, does not imply otherwise.

text Denotes the excerpts which have been reprinted from "Alcoholics Anonymous" 4th Edition (The Big Book)

To Members of Alcoholics Anonymous

My heartfelt thanks go to all those members who helped me beat the booze. Without their patience, support, and guidance I don't think I would be here today.

The parable at the end of my story inspired the style of the project, for it epitomises the conflict in my alcoholic mind. I am grateful to the A.A. member who shared it with me. I quote many "pearls of wisdom" I have heard in A.A. rooms but I do not betray anyone's anonymity, nor do I share anyone else's story. I have left out the locations and the names of those involved.

I do not seek to promote my recovery from alcoholism as the solution to anyone's problems for each of us must find our own peace. I merely relate my own story and try to show how my thinking has changed during my life and say. One day at a time it works for me.

To Suffering Alcoholics

The changes in me are by no means unique. I have seen it in many recovering alcoholics. I have not become a saint, and I am neither a Guru nor an expert. I'm just someone who was too proud and stubborn to seek help until it was almost too late. Fear became an asset when I realised I didn't want to die from my disease and that I couldn't beat booze on my own.

My fervent hope is that the suffering alcoholic who reads this can identify with some of my experiences, and with the way alcohol warped my thinking and arrested my emotional development. If you seek help while there is still time, you can enjoy the same changes.

The fangs of sobriety (Freedom, Acceptance, Normality, Gratitude, and Serenity) will replenish the good qualities lost to alcoholism. The difficult days can be handled, the good days enjoyed. The world can be a good place to be if you choose to get honest with yourself, change your attitude, and live in the day, not in your fears. But only you can make that choice.

For Families

To the families who, in a state of frustration and helplessness, struggle to come to terms with the irrational and despicable behaviour of the suffering alcoholic in their midst. I say do not despair, there is help at hand, but your loved one will only seek it when he has reached his own rock bottom. I am convinced that self centred alcoholics will not stay sober long term to benefit other people. Only the personal pain of living in the madness will force them to seek help.

I was a nasty, unreliable, arrogant, self centred liar when I was a drunk. My family loved me so they tolerated me and tried to help me. I let them down and embarrassed them many times.

My recovery has transformed me into a responsible and respected member of my family. I have the trust and love of all those closest to me. They have told me they are both proud of me and happy for me. If it can happen to me, it can happen for your loved one. I hope you have the same outcome my family now enjoy.

Prologue

My story describes the journey from childhood, through twenty years of alcoholic suffering to the present day, more than twenty two years since my last drink. There are no lies in this book and no exaggeration of the facts. I have tried to highlight the skewed thought processes from my early years, which I believe set me on the road to alcoholism.

Most alcoholics are not bad people. They are extremely self centred, hyper-sensitive, and very sick individuals who are incapable of recognizing their illness, and the damage it causes to them, and those closest to them. The fangs of alcoholism (Fear, Arrogance, Negativity, Guilt, and Selfishness) suck most of the good qualities from their consciousness.

When they reach the bottom of their personal pit of hopelessness, and have lost their dignity and the trust of their family and friends. The arrogance that blinded them from the reality of their condition is replaced by complete despair. At this point, for the lucky ones the survival instinct kicks in. If they admit that booze has beaten them, and are ready to change their thinking and behaviour, help is at hand.

At the bottom of my pit of hopelessness I sought help from Alcoholics Anonymous. The support of its members, coupled with the A.A. 12 step programme led me back to sanity. I learnt how to deal with both the good and the bad aspects of daily living without having to use alcohol, or any other drug as a crutch. I was shown how live with peace in my head one day at a time.

The Selfish Brat

My earliest memories of family life take me back to 1959. I was just five years old and the baby of the house. Sitting on the stairs sulking, I watched my father come through the front door, "what's for dinner" he called as he walked in.

A chorus of shush! met him from our neighbours, who had all piled into the living room to see this marvellous new invention called television. It was the first of its kind in our street, and had been installed while Dad was at work.

"This was for us, not the whole street!" I silently screamed to myself. Most kids are a bit selfish at five years old, I never grew out of it.

Dad was not so silent, he asked the neighbours to leave so he could get his dinner in peace. I smiled as I watched the neighbours leave, but quickly went back to sulking when he softened the blow by inviting them back later on to watch the telly. After dinner we all settled down and watched TV until bedtime. My tantrum at being sent to bed so the adults could watch TV earned me a slap on the legs. None of my brothers or sisters protested, but then they could tell the time and didn't miss the chance to wind me up.

"The squirt can't tell the time, it's already bedtime" they chanted, poor me nobody liked me. I cried myself to sleep whilst trying to think of ways to get my own back on my horrible siblings.

I didn't have to wait long. The field at the bottom of our garden was bordered by a stream that we were absolutely forbidden to go near, never mind try to cross to the other side. That Saturday Mum was busy cleaning and Dad was at work, my big brother and my two big sisters were playing dares in the field. "You can't play, your too small" they sneered. The dare was to jump the river. After a while they were all playing on the far side of the river, "Help me across" I yelled, "clear off squirt" came the reply.

The red mist descended and my chance for revenge became clear. I ran back to the house and told Mum what they were up to. The squeals and cries were music to my young ears, when my anger subsided I regretted having blown the whistle on my brothers and sisters.

I knew that my siblings wouldn't take kindly to my betrayal, but they didn't give me a hard time for long. They didn't hold a grudge the way I did. We were to have many wars through the years as most siblings do.

But I wasn't like most kids for I held on to my anger and frustration, and let it fester in me. The real conflict, the "Battle of the Wolves" within me had begun, and it still goes on today.

Life moves on and so did we, Dad got a new job and we had to move house, a big adventure for a five year old.

My new school was much bigger than the old village school. Although I made friends and fitted in, I never ran with the crowd. I was a bit of a loner who joined in just enough to be accepted. I was good at most subjects in school and enjoyed classes. To admit this was not the "done thing", so once again I did enough to get by without being noticed. Happy to secretly feel superior in the knowledge, that I found easy what my classmates struggled with.

It never occurred to me that if I helped them, they might like me more, after all this was my gift, why should I give it to them. The hidden arrogance and selfishness that came easily to me was turning me into a very mixed up kid. I didn't like myself very much, I was acutely aware of my small stature and big front teeth, which made me the constant butt of my classmates jokes.

I was always getting in trouble for being late home from school. Mum would ask "why can't you just come straight home like all the other kids". I'd shrug my shoulders and Mumble some vague excuse dreamed up on the spur of the moment, and would get a cuff on the lug for my trouble.

I wasn't up to mischief in these absences. I was John Wayne, Burt Lancaster or the Lone Ranger. Playing out the roles they depicted on the silver screen. On my way home from school I was lost in the wonderful world of my imagination. There I could be who I wanted and do whatever I felt like. I'm sure all kids probably visit these fantasy worlds often, but I was becoming a resident.

In truth I didn't know then that I was trying to escape the drudgery of responsibility and boredom that was life as I saw it. I longed for a life where nobody told me what to do or when to do it. A world where I didn't have to do chores or put myself out, a place where I could suit myself and not have to think of the needs of others.

During the summer holidays were the best times for me. My Dad worked on a golf course and I would spend many happy days helping him at work, or just messing about on the course with my brother.

The public swimming baths were just around the corner from our house, yet I never learnt to swim. I wasn't afraid of the water, I was afraid of what people might say when they saw this scrawny little runt in swimming trunks, self awareness ran riot in my head.

There was a terrible traffic accident involving a bus on the main road at the end of our street. This was just a few yards from our front door. There were lots of injuries and I think some people did not survive. We had several of the walking wounded in our house while they waited for ambulances to take them to hospital. I was very frightened when I saw some of the injured people.

My parent's example of selflessness and compassion for complete strangers made me feel proud, for I somehow knew they were doing what was right. But I also felt uneasy at the same time, for I neither felt nor understood these emotions.

After the people had all gone, Mum cried for the victims of the tragedy. I thought that was silly, why cry for someone you don't even know. At the tender age of Seven, I was bereft of compassion and self centred to the point where I resented my parents putting these people before me.

We lived two streets away from the home of Crusaders football club, many happy evenings were spent watching "The Crues" train, and dreaming of playing for them. But I couldn't support them, after all they were my Mum and brother's team, so I followed Linfield just to be awkward.

Not a wise move, my friends found out and while playing on the railway lines, which wasn't allowed, one of them disappeared only to return with my Dad. I heard Dad's shout and looked around to find that all my so called mates had vanished, leaving me to be frog marched home. The march wasn't to the tune of left right, left right, it was: SLAP-YAP, SLAP-YAP, whilst my one time friends sniggered from a safe distance.

Half a mile of humiliation later, it was no dinner and straight to bed. My Dad loved me, but the shock of seeing me in such danger had sent him temporarily insane. What goes around comes around, I now knew how my brother and sisters must have felt, when two years earlier I had spilled the beans on them, when they left me on the wrong side of the stream. I probably deserved what I got, but you couldn't have told me that.

I hated the world and everybody in it, "fuck the lot of you" was the thought in my head when I cried myself to sleep that night. I never got the chance to get revenge on those one time friends, who were now the world's biggest assholes in my eyes.

My Dad had gotten fed up with the wet weather and had accepted the offer of a job. It looked like we were on the move again. This time it wasn't going to be a bus ride across the city, we were emigrating to Australia. I was ecstatic to be leaving this once happy environment which had so recently turned on me. I looked forward with excitement to this latest chapter in my young life.

Everything was settled and all the arrangements made for our trip around the world. But that wonderful invention, that had me sulking at the start of my story was about to throw a spanner into the works. Television played a big part in our young lives, and when Mum watched a programme about snakes, crocodiles and spiders in the "land of OZ", she immediately declared that if we went to that country it would be without her.

She was adamant, persuasion and cajoling proved a waste of time, bullying and threats washed off her like water off a ducks back.

The fact that Dad had given notice to quit his job made no difference, "Find another job" she told him. Indeed if the "Wizard of Oz" himself had appeared in a cloud of smoke and flames to declare Australia safe to live in, she wouldn't have changed her mind. The future looked very bleak to my young eyes.

From that day forth my Dad hated the television with a passion, it didn't stop him watching it though. The ritual of complete silence while he checked his football coupon on Saturday continued for many years thereafter.

Dad did find another job and we "emigrated" fifteen miles down the road to a small village in County Down, where Dad took charge of yet another golf course. A modern three bedroom semi with gardens front and rear was part of the deal. I thought my Dad must have won the pools when I first set eyes on what was a fabulous mansion to a seven year old. The only grass in our old street in Belfast fell off Dad's boots when he came home from work.

I was blissfully happy with my new surroundings, and was positive that I would really enjoy life in this quaint little village.

Dad's work was only two minutes walk from the house, the golf course was surrounded by hundreds of acres of woodland for me to explore. A new young sister had been added to the clan just before our move out of Belfast, another one came along shortly after we moved to our new home. I thought the stork was extremely clever to be able to follow us as we moved from place to place.

Dad was busy with his new job, Mum was engrossed in looking after my young sisters. I was no longer the baby of the house and that suited me just fine, left to my own devices I explored my new surroundings with great enthusiasm. Negativity was banished from my thinking. I even managed to be nice to people most of the time.

As "blow-ins" we were not readily accepted in the village but it didn't matter, I was in my element on my own playing in the woods. Or going to the ruins of a once majestic old mansion, which served as a castle full of knights, or a fort under siege by apaches, life was very good indeed.

The village had a small school beside the church. There were only seven of us in my class, unlike my previous school I felt comfortable showing off my abilities in the classroom. My former school had been more advanced when it came to penmanship.

I was constantly in trouble for doing joined writing, but it boosted my confidence to know I was ahead of the game. I was streetwise enough to know not to belittle others with less skill in the classroom, for I was very small for my age, and hated fighting because I was no good at it.

The following term was year five, my new teacher was great, with a quick wit and total commitment to his pupils. He taught me for the rest of my primary school years, they were by far the happiest years of my education.

Life away from school was good, initially shunned as blow-ins we had been accepted and had made good friends in the village. I played little part in this transition, but benefitted from the outgoing nature of my brothers and sisters. Golf and football were the two main pastimes, we would play for hours on end, when the light failed hide and seek took over.

Golf provided more than just fun, there was money to be made selling golf balls, and caddying for the well heeled members and visitors who frequented the club. Being the greenkeepers son had its advantages, I would often get to caddy for good payers because of who I was.

This was a double edged sword for it didn't go down well with some of the other caddies. One in particular who was in my class at school, but was twice my size was very annoyed at the preferential treatment I received.

He bullied me at every opportunity, stole my hard earned cash, and threatened me with all kinds of horrors if I squealed on him, or if the money was not forthcoming.

To my eternal shame fear drove me to stealing to keep him off my back. However I wasn't a thief and my shame gave me the courage to tell him to piss off in front of his friends. He beat the crap out if me, but I still refused to steal for him. I had earned his respect, we eventually became good friends.

The good things going on in my life had changed my thinking, I now had a positive attitude, I played the accordion in the local band, I was in the Boys Brigade, I went to Church and Sunday school, played football and loved going to the youth club.

Dad took up sea angling when I was about ten years old, I went with him and I loved it, sea angling became my obsession and he was no longer just Dad, he was my friend.

He was struck down by the chicken pox, how could this happen, what was I going to do if he died. It was a great relief to me when I found out that chicken pox wasn't life threatening. However it was certainly causing my Dad great discomfort, The short fuse of his temper became even shorter when the itching was very bad.

He shaved his head so that he could scratch it more easily. He didn't appreciate the doctor's observation that Yul Brynner had nothing on him. "I don't think it's funny" he told him, it would have been a far less civil response if the doctor hadn't been a member of the golf club.

I also got infected and was confined to the house, this was a disaster for I was going to miss the scripture knowledge exam in school. On the day of the exam I sneaked out of the house and attended school, the teacher foolishly let me stay, for he knew how much I loved all things Christian.

Most of the school went down with chicken pox and some of them blamed me, I didn't care for I had passed the exam. Top of the class in most subjects every year, my confidence was at an all time high when I got the grades to allow me to go to the technical college instead of secondary school.

The Apprentice Piss Artist

By the time I started the technical college, I was already part of the crew on one of the local angling charter boats. My wages were free fishing trips, and an education in both the ways of the sea, and of the sailors who worked on it. I was a normal happy child without a care in the world.

Mums wanderlust returned and although Dad stayed in the same job, we once again moved house. This in itself was not a major problem for me, I was now at school in the seaside town where I did my fishing, and we were moving to that very same place. Could things get any better?

No, but they could get worse. As crew on the boat we rarely returned to harbour early enough for me to catch the last bus home. This wasn't an issue for my parents, because the skipper would always give me a lift if I missed the bus. The skipper, being a thirsty sort of fellow always liked a beer after work. Although the pubs closed at ten o'clock, the pub at the pier had a side door in a different time zone for mariners and other privileged patrons.

The "Good Wolf" within was very much in control, but his alter ego was only sleeping and had not gone away. He was soon to awaken and renew the fight for control of my mind.

Night after night I would sit in the pub with my coke or orange soaking up the atmosphere, and the tall stories told by the anglers. The banter was great and I felt very grown up, even though the vast majority of my company were old enough to be my father.

After a while I wanted to try the magic potions that seemed to put a smile on the face of everyone in the pub. After much pleading with my companions and hardly tall enough to see over the bar, I began my drinking career with a pint of 3 parts lemonade to 1 part lager. The bar staff accepted me because of the company I kept, soon I graduated to pints of lager.

My Dad would have killed me if he had known what I was up to, but he was always in bed when I got home. By the time I was fourteen my regular tipple was rum, chased down by a pint of Guinness.

Not a normal healthy way for a schoolboy to quench his thirst. I had started on a path that would take me to dark and terrifying places in my head. Although my schoolboy drinking was unusual, I wasn't consuming vast amounts of booze. I was however drinking enough to be considered a regular in the pub at the pier.

My dubious hobbies left no time for homework or normal teenage socializing. I lost interest in healthy teenage pursuits and became an atheist to avoid wasting good drinking time in Church. Homework was done on the bus to school and in the playground.

Having a talent for mental arithmetic meant that I could do the sums in my head and write down the answers, showing no evidence on paper of how I reached the solutions. This got me in trouble with my teacher, when I told him I did the sums in my head, he called me a cheat and a liar in front of the whole class. "I want you back here after school", he said.

When I went back to the classroom for my detention he had written ten fairly difficult sums on the blackboard, he handed me a sheet with the same sums on it. "I'm going to do these sums on the board, turn your back to me and write the answers on your sheet".

I finished when he was still on number seven. My answers were all correct, with no rough work in sight. My smug look earned me a growled get out of here, "up yours" I thought. The following day the teacher apologised to me in front of the class.

My grudging respect for his actions did not assuage my resentment at being humiliated in the first place. Forgiveness wasn't something I was familiar with.

I told my two best friends in school about my drinking habits, of course they never believed me. How dare they question my honesty, the gauntlet was thrown down the challenge accepted. I would prove to them that I wasn't lying.

The next night the three of us went to the cinema to watch a James Bond film. Afterwards I insisted that we go to the pub at the pier. None of us had any money left but that didn't matter, we walked up to the bar and I asked them what they were having in a fashion I had heard many times in this place.

Like two scared rabbits, they scanned the shelves and finally picked their poison. I called Jimmy the barman over and ordered a pint of Guinness for me and two bottles of piper for the lads and put it on the slate.

Jimmy threw a fit and said "what are you doing bringing these youngsters in here, do you want to get me sacked". I casually replied, "I've a point to prove in school, just a quick one and were on our way".

We got our drink, both "these youngsters" were 6 months older than me, and 6 inches taller than I was back then. It was the talk of the school for days, I got nods of approval from my classmates and older boys alike. My confidence was at an all time high. My ego soared, this little squirt had street cred at last. Drink had given me one hell of a buzz.

Luckily the only teacher who found out was an angler who often drank with me in the pub at the pier. The "Bad Wolf" within was stirring from his slumber, he was starting to eat away at all the good things in my head. Although I didn't realise it, I was already well on my way to becoming an alcoholic.

I was also becoming quite the little entrepreneur. In the last two years before I left school I had started shoplifting to feed my drink habit. I would lift anything I could sell to my school mates, I even took orders, and in my warped state of mind I took great pride in coming up with the goods. I was very good at this, and as my reputation grew I was even challenged to a shoplifting contest by another pupil. He was doing this for a dare, but to me my credibility was on the line.

He never even came close to my haul, and was a nervous wreck for days, worrying that someone might find out, unlike me, he had a conscience.

Having perfected the art of doing enough to get by in primary school, it was easy for me to hide my drinking from most of those close to me. To an outsider I appeared normal, nothing had changed. As the drinking increased the only person I was able to fool was myself.

Dad had become aware of my drinking, at first I think he put it down to youthful experimentation. When he realised this was not the case, and that I was already a hardened drinker, he tried everything short of locking me up to break the habit. The rows were frequent, the promises I made were always broken. What harm was I doing, why can't they leave me alone.

In my arrogance I decided that nobody had the right to tell me what to do. Dad was no longer my friend. I didn't realise that my family were concerned for me, and that I was breaking my parent's hearts. I hadn't even left school, but I wanted to leave home. In my lucid moments I was ashamed of what I was becoming.

As had always been the case, I did enough in school to achieve acceptable grades. I left at Easter, just after my fifteenth birthday. I wanted to work on the golf course, for I was already familiar with the work, Dad said I should get a proper trade. I accepted his advice and started working as an apprentice motor mechanic in a local garage.

Things were tight at home, Mum needed another pay packet coming in, and I needed money for drink. I earned the princely sum of £3.7s/6d per week. Mum took the £3, my bus fare to work took the rest. I got my drink money by caddying, and working on the boat. It was never enough, I needed a job that paid better.

The mechanics in the garage were teaching me nothing, all I did was fill petrol tanks and wash cars. This was a plausible excuse to quit serving my apprenticeship and go after better wages. I got a job in a shop that paid £7. I told Mum it paid £6 and voluntarily contributed an extra pound to the housekeeping, what a dutiful and caring son I was turning into. That stroke won me some much needed brownie points, at least for a short while. I didn't like my new job, but the pay was good so I tolerated it.

Whilst working here I had my first experience of personal grief. My Mum phoned me at work to tell me that my oldest sister's baby son had passed away. They said it was a cot death, I was devastated and my boss brought me home in his car. This tragedy bolstered my belief that there was no God, for what God would visit such suffering on our family. I kept a low profile during the next few days.

I couldn't handle the pain of grieving so I shut it out, as I did with any emotional trauma. Not once did I think about what my poor sister and her husband must have been going through. I didn't know anything about dealing with life's problems in a mature way.

Alcohol had arrested my emotional development. I was destined not to start to grow up until I stopped drinking twenty years later. Such is the power of alcohol.

Another job opportunity came up in a factory close to home, it was for an apprentice sewing machine mechanic. I applied and was interviewed on a Saturday morning and told I could start after working my notice in the shop. I duly gave a weeks' notice on Monday morning.

Imagine my trepidation when I got the phone call telling me there had been a mistake, and that the new job had already been taken. I had to eat humble pie and ask to keep my current job, much to my relief my boss kept me on. My gratitude to him was quickly forgotten, when two weeks later the same factory offered me the apprenticeship again. I couldn't understand why he was so upset with me. Needless to say when I gave notice this time there could be no going back.

Two more children had been added to the clan, I now had another young brother and baby sister. By this stage I knew the stork didn't deliver the babies. I was becoming aware of the opposite sex and teenage hormones were, playing havoc with my thoughts. For short periods the natural sexual urges of youth, displaced my craving for alcohol.

But the urge to drink was much too strong and it invariably took me away from normal teenage activities. I was happy to let this happen for I still couldn't see the problems drink was causing for me.

I started in the factory and got on well with my new colleagues. I liked my new job fixing the sewing machines, I liked the young girls who worked them even more.

I was too shy to ask them out, they were not shy at all. Soon I was going on dates and going to dances like any normal teenager, but my early attempts at romance didn't go well. I fell deeply in love with every girl I went out with. I then proceeded to get pissed and totally forget about her, no wonder the relationships didn't last very long.

My other major interest during my teenage years was the accordion band. This was a great way to socialise and there was always drink to be had at these gatherings. There were good looking girls in the band, and even an ugly little squirt like me had a chance to pull when I was in the band uniform. For some strange reason girls followed the band, when the parade would stop for a break, female company was easy to find. I had no more success here than I did with the girls from the factory.

My social skills had been learnt in a pub full of old men. I was out for what I could get and didn't know how to treat a girl properly. In their eyes Davy wasn't boyfriend material.

In frustration I would seek solace in drink, even that was difficult with an older brother and sister in the band. Why couldn't they leave me alone?

By the age of seventeen my drinking friends were telling me to ease up on the hard stuff. I laughed at this, sure I only took an occasional rum or whiskey, I usually stuck to Guinness. I honestly believed the rubbish I was spouting, what I now know to be alcoholic blackouts hid the memory of what I drank from my conscious thoughts. Not remembering what happened the night before was par for the course for most of the people I drank with. As far as I was concerned it was part of the normal cycle for social drinkers to ask "How did I get home last night?"

I had sprouted up and was now nine inches taller than when I left school. Dad was at the end of his tether, he told me that if drinking got me into trouble I couldn't expect any help from him. That was music to my ears, perhaps he would leave me alone now, life looked good again.

The first sign that drink was affecting me differently from my teenage friends occurred at a band parade when I was seventeen. My friend had procured a half bottle of gin from somewhere. He tried it but didn't like it, so he passed it to me. I was standing on the back of a flatbed lorry at the time. I don't remember what happened next, but my friend told me I took a large swig from the bottle and fell to the grass in a heap.

This was the first time I had blacked out almost instantly after taking a drink. That night I wondered if maybe there was something wrong with my drinking. This was quickly dismissed as utter nonsense, I was far too young to have a drink problem.

I continued to socialise with my workmates, the normal routine was to meet in a pub to get loosened up with a few pints, before going to the dance, for there was no bar in the dancehall. The closest watering hole to the dance was the pub at the pier, I rarely made it to the dance, on the few occasions that I did, I was nearly always too drunk to be let in. I thought I was destined to never find a steady girlfriend, but the factory came to my rescue.

They transferred me to a different site, there I met a girl called Shirley. She was good looking, funny, and intelligent so why she fancied me was a total mystery. However, they say that love is blind and we started dating, we got on really well and the time I spent with her kept me out of the pub. She came from a family well used to hard drinking, so me taking a few pints was no problem, indeed she liked a drink herself. Shirley became a regular guest in our house, my parents were delighted to see I was finally settling down.

We attended my sister's wedding and were teased that it would be our turn next. We made no attempt to argue against them, for we would happily have walked down the aisle together there and then. She does not know how lucky she was to escape that future. I thought I was in love with this girl, but I never knew the meaning of the word.

Shortly after that day I went out for a drink with a mate. We left the pub slightly the worse for wear, but certainly not drunk. Taking our unfinished pints with us, we went down the main street with drinks in hand. I noticed two policemen approaching us and we made a run for it, we rounded the corner, put our drinks on a window sill and ran into a nearby dark alley, we had lost them. When we thought the coast would be clear we left the alley, chuckling to ourselves as we headed back to the bright lights.

We walked straight into the arms of the law. In the cop shop I told them I was eighteen, for I almost was and I didn't want my Dad to know about this. We were to be charged with theft of a glass from the bar, simple drunk and assault.

We protested vehemently to the charge of assault, for we hadn't assaulted anybody.

One of our glasses had fallen from the window sill, spilling its contents on a bystander, this was deemed to be assault. We sobered up quickly when we learnt our fate was to be an appearance in court, they sent us on our way with our tails firmly between our legs. My Dad would have to know about this, but how could I tell him. I didn't have to for the police arrived at our house the next morning, they had found out that I was under age so the charges were amended accordingly. All hell broke loose when they left, I'd never seen my Dad so angry.

I took it on the chin for I knew I was out my depth and needed help to deal with this. I remembered him telling me a few short months ago, that if I got into trouble I could hang by my own tail. I had a fear in me like nothing I'd ever felt before. Back in those days a word in the right ear could fix these relatively minor misdemeanours. My Dad loved me unconditionally, he got the charges dropped.

I was humbled and grateful for his help, we talked at length about my drinking.

He told me I was heading towards being an alcoholic, and that my girlfriend would probably ditch me if I didn't wise up.

I resented this comment for she wasn't a shallow person, she loved me and would stick by me. For the first time I admitted to myself that drink might be a problem. I agreed with him that excessive drinking would bring me nothing but trouble. I promised to control my behaviour and I meant it.

There was a serious flaw in my commitment, neither of us understood the true nature of alcoholism. It was not drinking to excess that caused my troubles, it was any drinking at all. It was the first drink that set off the obsessive craving that wouldn't allow me to control my drinking. My girlfriend was not amused with my antics, but didn't give me a hard time. A few weeks of best behaviour later I turned eighteen. I could now drink legally, it wasn't long before the piss artist returned with a vengeance, my drinking was worse than ever. New thoughts invaded my head, if I knew that drinking the way I did would lead to trouble, why did I keep on. Fear and guilt brought out the nasty side of my nature.

My Dad was right, when Shirley seen this side of me a few times, she told me I changed into a bastard when I was drunk and ditched me.

From Madness to a Fresh Start

I was inconsolable, and what made it worse was that I saw her every day at work. It took every ounce of my willpower not to burst into tears on the middle of the factory floor.

I didn't blame her for our break-up, for I knew that my conduct had driven her away. I asked for, and got a transfer to another branch just down the road. Self pity was now added to the poisonous mixture in my head, I thought of myself as a pathetic waste of space, I didn't care if I lived or died.

Eventually I could pass Shirley in the street without feeling too bad. I now spent most of my free time in the pub. Darts and pool were my hobbies, for they were only an arm's length from a pint. I went through a period of living with no ambition or motivation to do anything. The only reason I went to work was to get money for drink. The last of my social activities to bite the dust was the band.

The lads in work were organising a trip to Old Trafford to watch Man Utd play Chelsea. I needed something to get me out of this rut for I knew this was no way to live, so I put my name down for the trip.

As we boarded the bus to take us to the boat, the excited chatter was all about seeing George Best and Bobby Charlton. Someone put a can of beer into my hand, so I smiled and politely joined in. A coach load of friends couldn't stop me from feeling completely alone.

We boarded the overnight ferry to Heysham, but nobody went to bed. We stayed up playing cards and drinking all night. I don't remember much of the crossing. I do recall sitting in Heysham at seven in the morning, drinking scotch straight from the bottle. I must have gotten some sleep on the bus to Manchester and managed to make it to the match.

We stopped at the Morecambe Bowl dancehall on the way back to the ferry, I was too drunk to be allowed in. So I found a pub that wasn't so fussy and hit the whiskey. They had to come and get me when the bus was leaving. I reluctantly went with them, the next thing I remember was a very embarrassing awakening on the ferry as it approached Belfast. I was cold and wet, I had peed in my trousers. This incident did not go down well with my friends, they didn't fall out with me, I think they pitied me. I wasn't invited to any more of their social events, they steered clear of me if we met in a pub.

In my eyes they no longer wanted me around. I was at the bottom of the pit, what little dignity and self esteem I had left was removed. The visits to the pub became more frequent, alcoholic blackouts followed almost every heavy session.

I was slowly sinking into madness, this is the way alcoholism progressed in me. I was still a teenager, yet the "Bad Wolf" within was bleeding me dry and relentlessly taking control of my mind.

My family had moved back to the village where I had grown up. I now knew that I had a problem with drink, but I fooled myself into believing that a new social environment would help me regain control of my behaviour. I refused to contemplate the notion that I was no longer the apprentice. I was a time-served full blown alcoholic.

I went to a barn dance at a farm about five miles east of our village, as usual I got drunk and remember nothing until I came back to consciousness in the early hours, walking out of a town seven miles west of home.

In the early hours after another session I woke up and couldn't move, I was enclosed in some sort of metal box. In my drunken stupor I thought I was in a police cell, I was under the seats inside a bus.

I must have slithered down off the seat, out of sight of the driver, who had locked up and gone home. Yet again I had peed in my trousers.

The factory closed for 3 weeks holiday every July, so with a month's pay in my pocket I headed to a slightly more up-market venue for a few pints. There was a card school in progress at the back of the lounge, I'd played poker before but only for pennies. When someone dropped out I asked to join the game and as the drink went in the wit went out. I lost every penny I had. I was like a lamb to the slaughter, I didn't even have the bus fare home.

I was glad that I had given Mum her housekeeping before leaving home. It was bad enough that I was broke, it would be far worse if I had to tell her she was not getting any money for the next month.

Luckily for me the Dockers went on strike, with merchant ships stranded in Belfast Lough there was a small fortune to be made bringing the crew ashore for a night out, and taking them back to their ships when the pubs closed. At the last ship we called with on the return leg of this liberty duty, we always went aboard and partied until the early hours with the crew.

The boat must have known its own way home, for none of us were in a fit state to take it there, but we always got back to harbour safely.

During the day I would earn more money by transferring to one of the trawlers which were hauling bacon and eggs to Scotland. Whilst unloading in Portpatrick I was almost killed when a pallet of eggs fell from the unloading derrick, I was directly below and only the quick reactions of one of the crew saved me, as he rugby tackled me into a pile of nets on the deck, risking his own life in the process.

The winch had jammed and the derrick split and fell to the deck miraculously missing everyone, the eggs were all over the harbour. The trawler had to stay there for repairs, so I got a lift back home on another vessel. I couldn't wait to get back, for this was a great yarn to tell in the pub at the pier.

Dressed in a new suit bought with the proceeds of the holiday windfall I went to the firm's dinner dance. The following Monday I was called to the manager's office to explain my behaviour at the dance. I didn't know I'd done anything wrong, apparently in my usual drunken state I'd fallen on a table, which had collapsed sending drinks over most of the people seated around it.

I had then started a fight over a taxi outside, I didn't get sacked, but I started looking for another job. These are only a few examples of my escapades from this year long binge, I remember very little else from that time.

A reprieve from the madness came along when I went to work for a company that sold sewing machines. Nobody knew me here, maybe I could leave my past behind and start again. Anything would be better than the hell I was living in. I looked upon this as a chance to put my life back together. I put my best foot forward and tried to make a go of it

I passed my driving test and was given a company van to enable me to install new machines in factories all over the country. I had to control my drinking to make sure I kept my driving licence. No licence no job was the company policy. I behaved myself, only drinking at weekends.

As my head cleared from the fog of alcohol, some of the negativity dissipated and I started to feel a bit better. Never being in the same work place for long periods suited me, self confidence returned and I began to enjoy life again.

I still felt lonely, my sexual urges were re-awakened and I wanted a steady girlfriend.

This was not just about lust, Shirley had shown me the companionship and caring that also helps build a successful relationship. I didn't want Shirley, but I did want a good relationship. I was convinced that this was the only thing that would take away my loneliness.

A blind date brought me the partner I sought. A good mate of mine was dating a girl, but getting to her house involved either two bus rides, or a long walk. Too miserable to pay the bus fares, and too lazy to walk, he came up with a novel solution to his problem. He would arrange a date for me with her sister Emily, in return for a lift to their house. I balked at the thought of going on a blind date. What if she was ugly or I didn't like her. That was rich coming from me, I was no film star, and the girls were not exactly swooning at my feet. Cautiously wary of his assurance that she was a nice catch, I agreed.

The first date was to be in our local pub, I had broken my toe and was unable to drive. That night I met the girl who was to become my wife. It was not hard to break the ice, I had worked with her in the stitching factory, and I simply hadn't recognised the name when my mate had told it to me.

She was very attractive, but didn't say much, it had been a long time since I had dated, and my confidence was disappearing like a Scotsman when it's his round.

I don't even remember what we said or did that first night. Despite my nervousness I liked her, I had no idea where this meeting would take us, but I wanted to find out. At the end of the night I asked her if she would see me again, she said yes, I was over the moon.

My mate never did get his lift, for by the time my toe healed he had split up with the other sister. His loss was my gain, I was now seeing Emily very frequently, and things were going well between us. Once I was back on the road we were seldom apart. I sensed that our relationship was developing into something special. Having been hurt before, I was a bit frightened to over commit. This was not just fear being knocked back, I was far more frightened of where rejection might take me. I didn't want to go back to the madness I had so recently left behind.

Other problems I was not yet aware of were on the horizon. A storm was brewing in Emily's home which would eventually force us into a decision about our future.

Emily's parents had separated before I came on the scene, it was not an amicable parting and her mother now lived in England. I knew her father from my early drinking days, a nice man, always well dressed, civil and popular with all who knew him.

On the few occasions that I was in her house, her Dad was never there. Emily was usually out the door and into my van, almost before it had stopped. I thought nothing of this and was flattered by her enthusiasm to go out with me.

I didn't know her Dad disapproved of me because of my drunken history. He was trying very hard to get her to dump me. Being the oldest sister still at home, she felt a responsibility to her younger siblings. She didn't think they could cope if she was not there. Her Dad played on this in an effort to get me out of the picture. With no one to turn to, Emily withdrew into herself. She didn't stop seeing me, but I knew nothing about what was going on in her home.

She was changing, she rarely spoke when we went out, and didn't care where we went, or what we did. Our dates degenerated into hello, goodbye, with nothing in between, except me quizzing her about what was wrong.

Had I done something? Did I say something? Is there somebody else? Are you ill? These questions brought no coherent response. This was driving me crazy and I was worried about her. We both knew things would have to change if our relationship was to survive. Eventually she told me what was happening.

I was relieved to know that I wasn't to blame for her anguish, then came the rage. Of course he knew about my past, he had been part of it, for he drank as much as I did. How dare he judge me, could he not see I had changed my ways. Maybe he just doesn't want to lose his housekeeper.

I wanted to confront him, but Emily said she didn't want to have to choose between me and her family. I backed off when she said this, for I didn't want to lose her. The fear of losing Emily also made me realize the true nature of my feelings for her. I now knew that I was in love with her, and wanted to spend the rest of my life with her. This did not quell my anger, and I promised myself that whatever it took to free her from this control freak would be done. I was ready to fight for our future together, if she was going to have to choose, I would make sure she chose me.

I was blind to the fact that this man was only doing what he thought was right for his child. My devious nature took over and I embarked on a mission to make her Dad appear to be the bad guy. I went into the house when he was there, he didn't like it, but he accepted it. I was always civil and respectful and when I had him at ease, I started to push his buttons, I was good at this for I had always been a manipulative little shit.

I would get Emily to sit on my knee, or kiss her in front of him. As we were walking up her front path leaving for a night out, I would give Emily a friendly pat on the backside, and throw in some suggestive remark about the fun we were going to have, always loud enough for him to hear. Always flattering Emily and making her feel good about herself, whilst driving her Dad to distraction.

He never took the bait when I was there for I think Emily had told him not to make her choose between us, as she had told me weeks before. I'm sure he gave Emily a progressively harder time when I wasn't around. If that didn't happen then my plan was failing, for I was determined to force Emily to choose whilst perceiving me in the role of her knight in shining armour, and her Dad the villain.

As far as I was concerned all is fair in love and war, the prize was too precious to lose, therefore the end justified the means.

I know this was despicable behaviour, but I was fighting for our future, I feel no shame about it and make no apology for it. I would do it all over again rather than lose my lovely Emily. My plan worked and Emily left home and moved into a bed-sit. Neither of us realised that Emily had jumped out of the frying pan into the fire. That fire did not start to burn for quite some time hence.

Her Dad shunned us and would not even acknowledge us if we met in the street. He was hurting, and it took a long time before reconciliation was achieved.

Back then co-habiting before marriage was just not done by respectable people, I wanted to be accepted in the community so I continued to live with my parents. But the bed-sit was now my real home, I wasn't going to risk losing Emily so I asked her to marry me.

We had very little money and with her Mum living in England and her Dad not speaking to us, the wedding would not be a lavish affair. That didn't bother us, we were together and that was all that mattered.

My Mum and my sisters, along with Emily's older sister hijacked the arrangements for the big day and we happily went along with their plans. The sisters took care of the dresses, the reception was to be in the new lounge at our local pub with Mum supplying the food. Both families did everything they could to give us a good day.

Emily's Mum was coming over, her Dad refused to come using the excuse that he wouldn't go if her Mum was there with her new partner. I wanted him there for I knew that would make Emily's day complete. Her Mum's new partner offered to stay away if that would help and Emily's family tried to persuade her Dad, but it was not to be. My bride to be had extended the hand of friendship and it was ignored. I was sad for her but also felt relieved, for I was wary of what might happen at the reception when drink was taken if he had come.

We were married in the registry office in July 1976. I will never forget my feelings when I first saw Emily that day. She radiated happiness from every pore, I was both stunned and proud at the same time. The sisters had done a great job on the dress, hair and make-up, but it paled into insignificance against the beauty of her smile. I couldn't breathe, I thought my heart was going to take the buttons off my shirt.

I was the luckiest man who ever lived. I went through the ceremony in a trance. The rest of the day went well until about tea time, I hadn't had a stag night and my mates hadn't given me a send off into wedded bliss, as was the tradition.

When I went downstairs to the public bar they kidnapped me. There were four of them but I put up a good fight before they bundled me into the back of their car. They took off like a bat out of hell, with me still fighting in the back seat. I kicked the back window out of that old Cortina on the way up the road, they tried to placate me by saying nothing bad was going to happen to me. I was having none of it, and continued to struggle, we ended up on a country lane about two miles away, where they stripped me to my underpants and abandoned me to make my own way back.

I ran home and got dressed and returned to the pub, some of the older men told my mates they had gone too far, after all it was my wedding day, not my stag night. They saw the error of their ways and apologised, I accepted their apology for I knew there was no malice intended. I was determined not to let anything spoil our day so I went back upstairs to my bride, who by now was bound to be wondering where I'd gone.

I drank too much but the euphoria of the event kept me presentable. At about 9pm we were chauffeured to our humble bed-sit in my van, which had been decorated with boot polish, lipstick and toilet rolls in the accepted fashion of the time. I had too much drink taken to drive.

Shortly after getting in I decided to take myself off on my own to God knows where. My wife tells me that she had been worried about me, and had went out looking for me after changing out of her wedding dress.

Apparently I flaked out shortly after arriving back in the early hours of the following morning. I have to take Emily's word for this, for I remember nothing after getting out of the van when we first came home.

Poor Emily, my sweet whispers earlier in the day about a night of unbridled passion to consummate our union was not to be. She must have wondered what she had let herself in for by getting hitched to me.

Holding the record for the shortest honeymoon in history is not something to be proud of, but that's the way it was. This stuttering start to married life didn't spoil things and soon we were enjoying a happy life together.

Besides we had great fun making up for my absence on our wedding night. We were both in full time work and could afford to party at the weekends, and do all the things that young lovers like to do.

After a couple of months Emily and her father patched things up and we settled in to married life. We would never be allocated a house of our own while we had the bed-sit so we moved in with a friend to gain points on the housing list. We had a great time living there, but we didn't tell the housing people that.

To them we moaned about the lack of privacy, the over-crowding, anything we could think of to promote our cause. It worked, and the real home-building started when we were allocated an upstairs flat across the road from my parent's house. This was our first proper home.

Growing Pains

Like most young working class couples starting out, we furnished our house on the never-never, and bought our clothes from a catalogue. Back then banks were sensible, they would not lend money to people of our ilk, so if we needed a few pounds extra, the high interest loan companies were our only option. Within a year we were heavily in debt, but I didn't listen to Emily's concerns about this, sure we could afford to pay it back.

Emily suddenly started to sleep walk, I woke up in the middle of the night, to find her wandering sound asleep out on the communal landing. How weird I thought, and guided her back to bed. About a week later, when I was coming home from work, my Mum met me with the news that Emily had lost the baby. It was so early in the pregnancy that neither of us even knew she was expecting. I rushed in just as the doctor was leaving, to find my wife crying in bed.

I comforted her and tended to her, as a loving partner should, a couple of hours later she had fallen asleep. I went to the pub to drown my sorrows, with no thought of how she would feel, if she woke up and I wasn't there.

There was no funeral for there was nothing to bury. I did not feel much sense of loss, for there was no emotional attachment to something I didn't know existed, I assumed Emily felt the same.

Things started to go wrong at work. The textile industry was rapidly falling apart for it couldn't compete with cheap foreign imports. I saw the writing on the wall and knew it wouldn't be long before my job disappeared.

Luckily a job came up in a small knitwear factory, there was no company vehicle but the pay was good and it was close to home. After some training on the knitting machines I was put in charge of the place while the owner went out and sourced orders for us.

Emily started to sleep walk again and I told her to go to the doctor. I was right, her sleep walking was her unique early warning that she was with child, we were ecstatic but also worried after what had happened just a few months earlier.

The pregnancy went well and in mid December 1977 she went into hospital. The new trend with modern Dads back then was for them to be at the birth, Emily wanted me there and although a bit nervous, I wanted to be there too.

I stayed with her the entire day and there was no sign of anything happening. At about 10pm the sister told me my wife was nowhere near ready to give birth yet and suggested I should go home. She promised to ring me the minute there was any change and assured me I would have plenty of time to get there before the birth.

I was just through my front door when the phone rang, Emily was in labour. In a mad panic I ran down to the bus stop to catch the last bus. While I was waiting I thumbed for a lift. Much to my relief the first car stopped. When I told the driver what was happening he drove me straight to the doors of the maternity unit. I shouted my thanks as I ran up the steps, confident I had gotten there on time.

Emily was not in her ward and when I found the sister she congratulated me on the birth of my new son. I said "Oh shit! I was supposed to be there!" she replied, "Never mind you, we were nearly not there either!" They reckoned that from first contraction, my wife had taken about ten minutes to become a mother. Emily was sitting up having tea and toast when I saw her, my son was in perfect health and so was she. When I held him for the first time I was proud and happy, we were not a couple any more now we were a family.

Little did I know that our new son "Alexander" would provide Christmas dinner for us that year. Having spent all our money on new things for our son and on Christmas presents, we were relying on my Christmas wages and bonus to buy the groceries for the holidays.

My boss wasn't the decent chap I thought he was, on the payday before Christmas he never showed up with our wages, he had done a runner, the factory was finished. I went home penniless, I had put my new son's name in the Christmas draw in the pub, and he won the turkey.

I went to work on the golf course with my Dad, the wages were far less than I had been used to but the job was on my doorstep, it was secure and I liked the work. With only one very low wage coming in cash flow soon became an issue. I tried my best to provide for us and we managed to struggle on, broke but fairly happy.

Dad pushed as much overtime my way as he could, and if one of our household appliances broke down Mum suddenly needed a new one, and passed her old one on to us. I was grateful to them for their kindness, but the responsibilities of family life weighed heavily on me.

I found it difficult to handle the setbacks normal adults took on the chin, for I hadn't made the transition from adolescence to adulthood I had not yet started to grow up.

When Alex was two years old our second son Edward was born, we were again delighted but our income would never be nearly enough to cover our household costs. An upstairs flat was unsuitable for raising children and we were allocated a terraced house.

The strain was beginning to take its toll, I was no longer the nice husband my wife knew and loved. The more our debts grew, the more moody and bad tempered I became. I realised that I was gradually slipping back into my old ways. I was drinking too much, I tried to fight it for I knew I was on dangerous ground.

I didn't want to admit to myself that I was an alcoholic, even though I was now fully aware that I couldn't handle booze, and should avoid it like the plague.

We struggled on and I somehow managed to control the amount I drank, mostly due to the fact that there was no money for booze. I got some extra part-time jobs doing gardens and fixing sewing machines in a small factory.

This along with my full time work eased the burden and things got a bit better. I still wasn't back to my old self but I was managing to cope and trying hard to keep my drinking under control. I loved my wife and my two young sons.

When things got too much for me I'd look at them and think to myself, "don't go back to the madness you've too much to lose". This gave me the strength to re-focus and carry on the fight against drink.

Things were different now, I felt guilt when I sobered up after a session, this would bring out Mr nasty and I was becoming hard to live with. The craving for booze brought back the manipulative little shit from a past life I thought I had left behind.

I thought of no-one but myself, fear of losing control made me want to take charge of everything in my life. I was becoming a control freak, the fire that Emily had stepped into when she had left home was smouldering. The "Bad Wolf" within was awake.

When I was growing up there was lots of happiness and love in my family, but we were not overtly demonstrative, hugs and kisses were not an everyday occurrence, at least not with me.

When Emily needed the comfort of a cuddle, I usually mistook this as a signal for some fun between the sheets. If my advances were rejected, I sulked like the selfish brat I had been as a child. This ploy usually worked, for she didn't want to upset me in case I hit the booze.

As hard as I tried I could only shake off the shackles of feeling inadequate as a family provider for short periods. I started to hate myself and frequently wallowed in self pity and shame for the way I was treating my wife.

When Edward was seventeen months old Emily dropped an atom bomb on my world, she was expecting twins. My trepidation had nothing to do with Emily being pregnant, in fact the thought of doubling the size of our family in one go delighted me. In a lighter moment I thought to myself, that's what you get for doing it twice in one night. The problem was how in the hell was I going to be able to provide for them.

I had lots of sleepless nights trying to solve this dilemma, the only solution was to find a way to earn more money. I found the answer and shortly after the twins were born I joined the Police reserves. With the troubles raging, peelers were earning big money via unlimited overtime.

I needed a car for this job and managed to gather up enough cash to buy an old banger. After successfully completing my training, I was posted to a quiet little town just seven miles from home. I got on well with my new colleagues, and the take home pay even in a month with low overtime, was well over double what I had been earning previously.

With the financial pressure off, home life started to get better. Mr nasty was not seen so often, and the challenges of the new job took my mind off my problems. I was sure that I could return to being the loving husband I was before. With the addition of David and Lisa to the clan, home-life was hectic. I marvelled at the way my wife coped with four kids less than five years old, she truly was a wonderful mother.

My new job brought other bonuses, each station had its own recreation club, and the division also had a "rec" club. If you had children the "rec" clubs threw fantastic Christmas parties, with no expense spared on the presents in Santa's sack. If you played sports, you could get a day off to play golf, or a half day for football, lots of other sports we covered as well. The more everybody joined in, the more overtime was created, for the shifts still had to be manned.

This new career was far better than I had ever dreamed it could be. It wasn't long before I had a nice Alfa Romeo at the door, we were the perfect model of a happy family.

There was a down-side to this job which I wasn't aware of during those early months. It was shift work, and there was no guarantee that you'd get your rest days off. If you were told you had to work, you had little choice in the matter.

I rarely got time to spend with my kids, and they did not understand that when Daddy had been working nightshift, he needed peace and quiet to sleep while they were awake and full of energy.

I must state here that I have the utmost respect for the vast majority of the police officers I worked with. But for a small section of the force, the stresses of the job had created a strong drinking culture. I was more than happy to join this group, for it reminded me of my days in the pub at the pier. After work we would frequently end up in the pub, on late shift we could be found in the canteen, drinking the night away. Nightshift often turned into a session when things went quiet on the streets. I fooled myself into believing everything was fine, my wife and kids were well provided for, so I deserved a bit of "Me time".

I never stopped to wonder if my wife could do with a break now and then. I seldom had time for my family, and it was easy to use the excuse that we were busy at work. Alcohol was becoming more important to me than the welfare of my family, the love of my wife, or anything else life had to offer.

Drink driving was not considered the evil it is today, everybody took their car with them when they went for a night out. I was no exception, but the difference was, most people were not staggering about in a drunken stupor, when it was time to drive home. Many times I drove home both from social gatherings, and work far too drunk to be safe behind the wheel.

The irony is, that the one time I crashed the car, I was sober, and on my way in to work. It had been an extremely busy time, and I was coming off the back of almost thirty shifts, each for a minimum of sixteen hours, without a day off. I set off for another nightshift and at the carriageway near our village, I must have fallen asleep at the wheel.

I went straight on instead of turning right, and careered down a six foot slope into a ranch fence. I woke up still in the driver's seat, with a 6 x 6 fence post resting on my shoulder.

If I had been six inches further left, I would have been decapitated. Thankfully no one else was involved, but the car was a write-off. The police arrived, and they were friends of mine. They thought I was drunk and knew I would lose my job if this went to court. I only had very minor cuts and bruises, so they towed my car out of the ditch with their land rover, took both it and me home and reported me as sick.

This act of kindness proved costly for me. With no record of the accident, I was unable to make an insurance claim for the car. I had to go back to driving old bangers, for I couldn't afford to pay the finance on a car in the scrap yard, and another one on the road.

A few weeks later I went out with some of my old mates from the pub at the pier, I don't remember how I got home, but when I met them in the bar the next day, they asked if there was much damage to my car. I thought they were winding me up when they said I had taken them to my house, where we'd partied long into the night. I had then driven them home, going straight over the middle of a major roundabout instead of around it. When I next looked at my car, I found a lump of turf wedged into the front valance. I reckoned I must have a charmed life and learnt nothing from this.

I continued to drink and drive for the rest of my drinking career, without ever getting caught.

A brand new station had been built in a town only three miles from home, and I was lucky enough to get transferred there on the day it opened. I joined a good crew and soon settled in to the routine. Whilst out on patrol in the car we stopped at a set of traffic lights, a sleek looking sports car pulled alongside us in the right turn lane.

With the lights still red he turned right and sped away, we went after him and got him stopped when he was faced with a traffic jam further down the road. He was an arrogant individual, who showed nothing but contempt for the fact that we had dared to stop him, and was very annoyed when I told him I was reporting him with a recommendation to prosecute.

He told me it would never go to court and we sent him on his way. When I gave the case details to my section sergeant later that day, it was obvious that he recognised the driver's name. He told me this guy had very powerful friends and said he would back my recommendation if I wanted to proceed, but warned me that it could cause trouble for me.

I thought about the time my Dad had put the fix in for me, but I reasoned that I was a stupid young kid, this was an asshole who wanted to rub my nose in it, I asked him to go ahead, screw the bugger.

The case files mysteriously disappeared and so did I. A dirty transfer, to a dangerous station on the peace line in Belfast was my reward for trying to do the right thing. Disillusion was now added to my thinking processes, I resolved never to take another case.

This was easy because reserves were supposed to be employed on guard duties and other non-operational tasks. The only reason we were allowed contact with members of the public, and encouraged to deal with cases was to keep up morale, for it is was a long day doing nothing but sitting in a pillbox and opening gates.

The Dark Times

Although my drinking was out of control, I thought that the fact that I was still providing financial security for my family made me a good husband and Dad. I never stopped to think that my family both needed, and deserved far more from me, I was so self-centred, that I only ever thought of my own needs.

We would go out for family days at the beach or the park, but I was there in body only, I wanted the day to be over so I could go to the pub. I didn't really feel part of the family, and I had very little to do with the early years of my children's development. My wife was a single parent of four kids, saddled with a bad tempered juvenile delinquent for a husband, how she managed, and why she tolerated me I will never know.

The bad tempered juvenile delinquent was turning into a vicious monster, not fit to be in the company of decent people. My heavy drinking was followed by angry outbursts, and verbal abuse of my poor wife was now a regular occurrence at home. She would put up with it for a while and then round on me, this was all the excuse I needed to once again hit the bottle. It must have been a great relief to Emily when I went to work.

Deep down I knew that I was treating my family badly, I didn't understand that this was alcoholism, progressing towards complete domination of my mind. I hated my job, for I now considered my colleagues to be a bunch of yes men and hypocrites, who would do anything to smooth the path of their careers. Of course this was nonsense, but alcohol had so much control over my thinking, that I rarely looked at anything in a positive light.

Whilst on patrol at chucking out time one night, a street brawl developed outside a local club. The call came in for assistance, and by the time we arrived on the scene there were several other units present, including the dog section. The crowd turned on us and a female colleague was punched in the face. All hell broke loose and the dogs were sent in, they bit several people, everyone a peeler, the injury on duty claims would make embarrassing reading for the doggie crew. When things eventually calmed down we went back to the station and had a "stress relief" party. I don't remember driving home the next morning, but that was by now not unusual for me.

The sergeant was on my back about not taking cases, I related my tale about getting a dirty transfer the last time I had taken a case, and he assured me that would not happen on his watch.

I told him he was right because I was still not taking any cases, he was not happy but there was nothing he could do about it, so work continued as normal for the next few weeks. By now I had stopped taking my personal sidearm home with me, for I had never been comfortable having it in a house with children. I was also afraid of what I might do with it in a fit of rage, for I was having occasional thoughts of a suicidal nature when I was coming of a heavy session. The sergeant saw me put it in my locker just before leaving for home one night and gave me a severe dressing down, "you're in danger 24 hours a day, so you must keep your gun with you at all times" he said. Little did he know that the greatest danger I could see, was from myself. I took the gun home, but I left the ammunition in my locker.

The arguments continued at home, with me making vicious, stinging remarks, and Emily becoming ever increasingly withdrawn and subdued. I couldn't see it, but this was affecting Emily badly, for I had become a control freak like her father had been when we first met. Worse was yet to come, for although physical violence was something I detested, it would also be part of my alcoholism. I could no longer function without booze, the more I drank the worse I behaved.

If I didn't drink for a couple of days I would get severe shakes, and was unable to sleep. After a few drinks sleep would come, but once the drink wore off I would awaken. I used to curse the milkman for waking me up, but in truth I was always awake long before he arrived.

My workmates were aware of the sergeant's wish that I would take a few cases, after a traffic incident one of the senior men in my section offered to let me take the case to get the sergeant off my back. They did not realise that I didn't care what the sergeant, or anybody else thought of me, but I took the case, "anything for a bit of peace" I thought. The senior man did all the paper work, all I did was put my name to it, and submit it to the sergeant. He gave it the once over, complimented me on how well it was presented, and forwarded it to the powers that be.

A couple of weeks later the sergeant called me to his office and gave me a long list of nitpicky queries about the file. I only had one query, "Who does he know" I asked "what do you mean" he replied. "There is nothing wrong with the file, and you know it!" I spat back at him, with a venom usually reserved for my wife. It turned out that the offender was a solicitor with the DPP office.

I snatched the file from his hand, tore it in two and dumped it in his bin. He was speechless with anger. "If it had been the local coalman he would already have his summons" I said, and walked out of the office.

History had repeated itself, it's hard to believe that I could be stung like this twice, but that is what happened. My next transfer was to a town closer to home, so my outburst had done me a favour this time. I didn't see it as a favour though, my ego was bruised and my disillusionment was reinforced. This made me even harder to live with, the arguments with my wife now sometimes included physical abuse. Suicidal thoughts were often with me now.

I hadn't been brought up to treat people this way. Somehow I had to find a way out of the madness. I knew I needed to stop drinking, but no matter how hard I tried, I could only manage a few days or maybe a week, before I was sucked back into insanity.

After trying for years to kick booze out of my life, I was now close to giving up, and letting it take me to permanent oblivion, or kill me, and I didn't care which.

My new posting mostly involved guard duties on the dwellings of prominent people. Usually just two of us, with one in a vehicle, whilst the other patrolled the grounds.

The solitary nature of this gave me plenty of time to contemplate my personal situation. I would tell myself I had beaten booze before and resolve to renew the fight. I'd have an upbeat attitude for a few hours. However they were long shifts, and by the time I was due to go home, I would be wallowing in pathetic self pity.

Another session, followed by another fight when I got home. After one such session I tried to strangle Emily on the stairs. I don't remember this, Emily only told me about it recently, Thank God I was too drunk to succeed.

A fight broke out between two work colleagues, this had been brewing for several months. The two protagonists went down to the car park at the back of the station to settle their differences man to man while the sergeant was out of the station.

If we had known about the fight we would have intervened. We heard the screaming from inside the thick station walls, by the time we got there it was all over. The loser's face looked like a bag of blue potatoes and he needed hospital treatment.

The sergeant was recalled to the station and she went berserk. After sending the wounded party to hospital she interviewed us one by one. We had already agreed amongst ourselves to say nothing, for in truth we had only witnessed the aftermath. None of us had been present during the event. We eavesdropped as she interrogated each of us, threatening everybody with anything she could think of if she didn't get the answers she wanted.

I was last in the queue and such was her frustration at this point that she threatened to write a report that would ensure I didn't get a new contract if I refused to spill the beans. Police reserves were employed on a three year contract, getting a second term depended partly on appraisals of you by your station commanders.

Nobody was going to take away my job for something that had nothing to do with me. The red mist descended, if I was going out I would take her with me. I reminded her that everyone in the station had at one time or another tried to get her to split these two up, but she had refused to listen.

I told her that if she ruined my chance of a second contract, she would be reading about it in the Sunday papers. When she tried to counter my argument with "who do you think you are".

I told her I was a man with a family to feed who had nothing to lose. She then tried the softly-softly approach, saying she had to find a way to write this up so that nobody got into trouble. I told her that everyone was telling the truth. We had not witnessed the fight and she would have to take our words for that.

One of our section had suggested that this could be written up as a street brawl injury, with the phantom assailant having escaped apprehension. I made her aware of this idea, and she calmed done somewhat.

She was very young and only in her first year as a sergeant. When I told her she should listen to the senior constables more, if she wanted to learn how to handle men, she got her bravado back and told me not to push my luck.

I said "don't forget what I said about going to the papers, now fuck off and grow up" I left her in tears of disbelief, that quiet Davy could be so vicious, my colleagues were also in shock, for none of them had ever seen me angry.

This was all at the top of our voices, and the whole section heard everything. A few weeks later I received my offer of a second contract, which I gratefully accepted.

I hated the job, but where else could I get the money I needed to feed my addiction to booze. With the amount I was drinking, and not nearly as much overtime available, there was less and less money left for the home. We were back in debt, but I didn't care as long as I was left alone to drink. I had no consideration for anyone, and days without drink were few and far between.

After one session in the pub I came home to find I was locked out, I had forgotten to take my keys with me. Unable to rouse Emily, who must have heard me, but I don't blame her for not letting me in. I went around the back and smashed a small window with a brick. In my drunken state I ended up with a large, deep cut on my thumb. The saint that she is, my wife came down and tended to the wounds of her drunken asshole of a husband, even though she knew, that I was liable to fly into a rage, and blame her for my stupidity.

My cruelty was getting worse and becoming more frequent. If nothing changed, sooner or later I would do serious harm to someone. My shame and remorse for my actions was no longer enough. I had to find a way to regain control, for drink was now my master. The "Good Wolf" within had seen enough, the battle for my sanity was about to begin.

The Bottom of the Pit

Suicide now appeared to be a viable option, if I could not find a way to beat the booze. I continued to drink just as heavily, but managed to control my behaviour, mostly by staying out of the way as much as possible.

My wife got a part-time job, and I decided to leave the police, I hated every aspect of the job, I blamed the shift work, and heavy drinking culture for my extreme mood swings and bad behaviour. There was some truth in this, but the real problems were all between my ears.

I reasoned that although the money was great, it was of no use to us, if all I did was drink it. I had turned my life around once before by changing my environment, and when an opportunity to go back to work on the golf course presented itself, I jumped at the chance.

Back in a job I enjoyed did put me in a better frame of mind, but money was very tight, and we were deep in debt. I had to give up my car, and I couldn't drink as often as I wished. More money was needed, so I decided to go after promotion in my chosen career, by getting myself golf course management qualifications.

Through time, I climbed the management ladder, and eventually achieved my aim, by securing a course managers job at a very prestigious course in Belfast.

The next eighteen months would prove to be the toughest round of my fight against booze. With a new job which I loved, the fresh start would surely help me to once again put my best foot forward and get on with life. But the "Bad Wolf" within was not finished with me, he had controlled me for a long time, and was not going to let me down gently.

I was very successful in my new job, and was now back driving again. I had joined the newly formed "Greenkeeper's Association" and had even been elected as vice chairman. We would arrange various social and educational events for our members, as well as regular golf outings.

On the face of it I seemed happy, and everything in the garden was rosy. Things were a bit better at home, but we were still deep in debt, the happy face was not a true reflection of how I felt. My craving for alcohol was with me all the time, I was fighting hard and trying to limit the amount I drank, but it always beat me, and sent me on a binge, sometimes for days at a time.

I still didn't understand the true nature of alcoholism, and therefore did not realise that total abstinence was the only solution for someone like me. After work I could regularly be found in the Clubhouse, drinking with the members before driving home, old habits die hard.

Before long the occasional pint after work turned into heavy sessions, both in the clubhouse, and in my local when I got home. The brief boost I had gotten from being successful in my new career was rapidly dissipating. I was slowly being dragged back into the madness.

I never bothered to check the oil or water in my car, and the engine seized, there was no money to fix it, but luckily a car company was doing a deal where you could trade in any car as deposit on a brand new model. I towed the car to the dealership, and drove away in my brand new car.

History was repeating itself, for we were a "two car family," trying to be a "one car family". I was still paying off the one in the scrap yard, as well as the new one, how I got the finance I will never know.

The new car further perpetuated the myth that I was indeed doing very well for myself. But I knew I was losing the battle against drink.

Help sometimes comes from the most unexpected quarter, and so it was for me. My regular sessions in the clubhouse had come to attention of my boss, I had not caused any trouble, but some members disapproved of me drinking and then driving home.

My boss was not an employee of the club, his was an honorary position and the less savoury parts of his job would usually be handled by the secretary manager, thankfully not on this occasion. I had a very good working relationship with my boss, and we looked upon each other as friends, it was his compassion and friendship which prompted him to deal with me personally, rather than delegate the awkward task which lay before him.

He invited me for coffee at his house, gave me a lecture about my behaviour and banned me from the clubhouse. It was not a total ban, and nobody would know about it, providing I behaved myself I could still occasionally use the clubhouse bar on pre-approved visits, or for greenkeeper's golf outings. But after work sessions were no longer permitted, and he made it clear that I would lose my job if I defied him. It was the rest of our conversation which was to prove to be the first step on my road to recovery from alcoholism.

He shared with me his own experience with drink when he was a young man, it turned out that he was a hell raiser who regularly drank just like me.

He had been lucky enough to realise drink was giving him trouble, and had stopped before it had taken over his life, as it had now done with me. We swapped stories for a while and he suggested that I would be far better off if I stayed away from drink altogether.

I told him I knew he was right, but did not think I had any more fight left in me. "Monty was a great general, but he always had an army to help win his battles" he said. He suggested I should get help with my battle. This was the first time that I had honestly talked about my drinking with someone who had been there, and knew what the madness was like.

I was impressed by the fact that he was prepared to take me into his confidence in such an unselfish manner, with his only motive being to help me with my problem. His words about "Monty" kept coming to mind and I wondered if maybe there was somebody who could help me, for I knew I had no chance on my own.

Somewhere in the fog of my drinking career Alcoholics Anonymous had been mentioned, although I knew nothing about these people I decided to contact them for help.

It took another couple of serious benders before I rang Alcoholics Anonymous. With a bad case of the shakes I answered the door to find two nice old gentlemen smiling at me. This was all I needed, for I thought these were a couple of evangelists, here to save my soul. I was about to slam the door in their face, when they told me they were from Alcoholics Anonymous.

I let them in and we talked in a similar way to my talk with my boss. They were very kind, and once they established that I had no drink taken, they shared some of their experiences with me. From what we shared I was now totally convinced that I was an alcoholic. I couldn't understand why they seemed so happy, but they were in recovery, I was still suffering.

They told me that it was the first drink that gets you drunk. If I was an alcoholic only total abstinence could give me peace. After we had finished our talk, they asked me if they could come back and take me to a meeting that night.

I asked them where the meetings were held, and told them I could make my own way down and would definitely be there. They gave me some literature and left me another phone number, telling me to ring if I wanted picked up for the meeting, or if I felt the urge to drink.

I fully intended to go to that meeting, but as the hours slowly rolled by I convinced myself that although these were nice people, the meetings were not for me.

My arrogance told me that now that I knew what was wrong with me and had the literature to help me, I could beat this on my own. I went forward with renewed hope and resolved to never drink again. The craving for drink left me and the relief was such that I was on a permanent high the like of which I had never experienced before. My new found zest for life made me easier to live with, more efficient at my job, and better able to cope with life's problems.

This temporary respite did not last for long. I didn't realise that for me to recover from alcoholism I was going to have to completely change my thinking. I needed to have my personality stripped away and re-built if I was ever to get lasting peace in my head.

Alcoholic blackouts were no stranger to me for they followed almost every heavy session. I was soon to experience a different type of blackout which did frighten me. Five or six weeks of my new found euphoria, with not a single craving for drink had me feeling great.

I was confident my troubles were behind me, and thought I had conquered the booze. After locking up at work one evening, I headed for home, it was a forty five minute drive home in the rush hour, but I remember nothing of the journey.

My next recollection was of me standing in my local with a drink on the bar arguing aloud with the invisible man. "You know better than to drink this"–"sure one won't do any harm" was the nature of the argument.

The other patrons must have thought I'd lost my marbles, they were right. Sanity almost won, for I left the bar to go home in my car, only to discover I had already taken my car home, before going to the bar in the first place.

I returned to the bar and got pissed, with the invisible man my only company. Somehow my subconscious had blotted out the positivity that had kept me away from booze for those few weeks and I was dragged back into the madness.

The "Bad Wolf within was trying to regain control. If it was bad before, this nightmare was ten times worse, the "Good Wolf" within was wide awake and came at me with fangs and claws bared. This would be the final battle before I found my army to help me fight this disease.

Having found a crumb of decency within me, my conscience wouldn't let up. Don't go there, you should know better, think of what you're doing to your family. Thoughts along these lines invaded my mind, it didn't stop me drinking, the craving for alcohol was too strong. The battle in my head was driving me crazy. The only way I could get any peace, was to seek complete oblivion in drink.

I didn't realise it but the visit to my home by the members of A.A. had sown the seeds of sobriety within me. The little knowledge I had gained from them, and from reading their literature, left me with no excuses for my behaviour. There was help out there, I just had to find the courage to lift the phone and ask for it.

I went to work and wandered around like a zombie, my staff kept me in a job, for they covered for me many times as I made more and more mistakes, or wasn't there when I was needed.

I went to bed at night wishing I would fall asleep and never awaken, only to find I could not sleep in case I got what I wished for.

I was back to sleeping only when drunk and awakening as soon as the drink started to wear off. I didn't care if there was money for my family's needs, only money for drink was important.

I would get a couple of days dry but would suffer severe shakes, on one occasion while lying in bed, I calmly watched as my ceiling filled with shadowy beetles, I hoped they had come to devour me.

I'd always had an abundance of long hair and in moment of drunken bravado I had my head shaved to support the noble cause of children in need that year. I was due to make a speech to promote the greenkeeper's association at a seminar the following week. I was embarrassed beyond belief, for skinheads were considered to be thugs back then. I managed to get through it safe in the knowledge that I could hide in the bottle later.

The following night I went to the pub, I remember nothing until I woke up the next morning with a terrible hangover, I rarely suffered from headaches coming off drink, but my head was thumping and the shakes were very bad.

I asked my wife what time I came home at, and she looked at me with a puzzled expression on her face. I said I must have had a very heavy session if my hangover was anything to go by. She told me I'd only been out for about thirty minutes, and had come home sober for a change and went to bed. I didn't believe her, but a conversation with the barman later that morning confirmed her story.

I'd arrived at the bar, ordered a pint and after a couple of mouthfuls had left to go home. I could no longer hold my drink, the need was worse than ever, but I didn't want to drink. Unable to satisfy my craving, I forced myself to drink against my will. Seven months had passed since my argument with the invisible man, I was at the end of my tether.

After forcing myself through one more weekend binge, I found myself sitting at home on Sunday morning, feeling empty inside. Loneliness, and utter despair hung over me, fear of what was going to happen to me invaded my brain. I knew I couldn't drink, yet how could I live without it.

The shakes were terrible and my heart was pumping like a jackhammer. I was jumping from chair to chair, a nervous wreck close to tears. Suicide once again looked good to me.

I was back to believing that I was a waste of space, and the world would be a better place without me.

The memory of two nice old men floated into my mind, in desperation I lifted the phone book and found the number for Alcoholics Anonymous. Following a garbled conversation about needing help, the voice on the end of the line told me there was a meeting about to start that morning.

I never even hung up the phone, my wife probably thought I was away to the pub, but thankfully that was not where I was headed. I drove the three miles to the meeting room with only one thought in my head. "If this doesn't work it's the nuthouse or the grave".

That thought is still with me, and it is as true today as it was when it first popped into my head over twenty two years ago. I went into the room without having the slightest idea of what lay ahead of me. But there was no fear, for whatever was to come, could not be worse than the way I was existing now.

Dry Doesn't Mean Sober

There were only a few people there, but they were very sympathetic, and gave me a cup of tea. They told me I was the most important person in the room, for I reminded them of where they had come from. I certainly didn't feel important, and burst into floods of uncontrollable tears.

In my mid-thirties, I was sitting there blubbering like a little child, and being comforted by a girl at least ten years my junior. With my billiard ball haircut and shaking like a leaf, I must have been a pathetic sight to behold.

I recognised one person in the room, a very successful businessman, surely someone of his standing could not be an alcoholic. How little I knew about this disease, I didn't even know it was a disease.

I calmed down eventually and managed to share a little of my troubles. They shared back with me, and explained some of the basics about A.A. and how it could help me. They told me to not take one drink for one day, and keep coming back. Get phone numbers from A.A. members and if the urge to drink returned, ringing someone before lifting a drink, would help me through.

Get on the programme of recovery. Many meetings make it easy, few make it hard, none make it impossible, they said.

There was something about these people that attracted me, they seemed to have peace and an understanding of a troubled mind like mine. I somehow knew this was the right place for me. I left that meeting with a tiny grain of hope that I could get the help I needed, and a list of meetings in the area.

These were the first building blocks of a recovery that would prove far more difficult than I could ever have imagined. All the things they had told me were ringing in my ears for the rest of the day. I couldn't wait to go to the meeting that night.

I told Emily about the meeting and how I had at last found people who could help me beat the booze, she didn't say much for I'd promised many times to mend my ways. My track record had made a cynic out of the most tolerant and forgiving person I'd ever known, her silent scepticism was understandable. I had no urge to drink but I'd experienced this before and I was under no illusions about my ability to return to my old ways. I knew I needed to stick close to A.A. if any good was to come of this.

I returned to the meeting room that night still very fragile, but clinging tightly to that little bit of hope from earlier. The room was packed with people, and I was again given a warm welcome by everyone.

The person presiding over the meeting is known as the secretary, at the start of the meeting he welcomed everyone, and announced that this was my second meeting. He told me this was my most important meeting, for having seen what was on offer, I had come back.

Most of the people who shared that night directed at least some of their comments towards me, they shared about their drunk stories and the early days of recovery. It was always the same messages. You're no longer alone, keep coming back, you're not a bad person, you suffer from a disease. It's the first drink that gets you drunk.

I heard them but I wasn't taking anything in for my mind was racing like a spin dryer trying to comprehend what they said. My brain was frazzled but it didn't matter for I was just happy that I wasn't in the pub. There was a big picture on the wall with the "Twelve Step Programme of Recovery" printed on it, many of them referred to this as my only chance to beat the booze.

I read some of the steps" during the meeting and I could see some logic in it, but it mentioned God and that was a taboo subject with me. The first half of the first step said "We admitted we were powerless over alcohol", I'd fought drink hard for many years, and had no trouble accepting this. It took a long time before I moved beyond that point.

I also met an old drinking buddy that night, a man who was as mad as a hatter when he took drink. What I saw now was a totally transformed person. I wanted what he had, and after the meeting I shared with him one to one. I left the meeting still fragile, but in a good frame of mind, for knew that I had found my army.

I attended A.A. meetings every night that first week, but inside my head there was a raging torrent of self doubt, guilt and fear. Although negativity still dominated my thoughts, there was also hope, the urge to drink had not returned and the relief of not having to drink, kept despair at bay.

Work was no longer about turning up and going through the motions. I started to apply myself to the job in the way that I had done when I'd first started. Progress was slow, I was out of condition and the physical side of the job wasn't easy.

Within a few weeks some of my staff could see a slight change in me, one of them told me it was good to have me back. This simple statement bolstered my confidence and helped me continue to fight off the negativity in my addled brain.

I shared my doubts and fears with an old hand in A.A. and asked for his help to sort out my head. He told me he had the same feelings when he first came around, he suggested that I needed to change my thinking, and that everything I thought I knew about how to live needed to be wiped from my brain, if I was ever to have a manageable life.

"The twelve step programme is a guide to living a decent way of life, and you need to get on with it". I couldn't understand this, "my life is manageable, it's only when I drink that things get on top of me", I replied. "Drink is the symptom, your misguided attitude is the problem"

I was not ready to listen, and didn't have a clue about the principles behind the programme of recovery. He told me to try to be patient, "You're obviously not stupid, the penny will drop if you keep coming back" he said. I was desperate to find the secret to the peace I saw in these people, I continued to ask questions of everyone who seemed to have the happiness I sought.

In my naivety I believed there was some magic answer that would take away all the pain of living, and give me what they had. No wonder he scolded me like a child, emotionally that's exactly what I was. It's hard being a juvenile delinquent in the body of a 35 year old man.

The growing pains would be severe over the next few years. My first meeting was in mid November, it would soon be Christmas and I didn't know how I was going to cope with the party scene, the craving for alcohol had still not returned, but I was convinced it would when the festive season came around.

My new friends told me to stick close to A.A. and I would be alright, they also suggested I should confide in my close family about my drink problem, and tell them not to offer me any booze, or buy me any for Christmas.

"It's the first drink that gets you drunk, so make staying off one drink for one day the most important thing in your life", they told me. Good advice, which I followed to the letter even though I didn't think it would work. I could see no other option, and was frightened that I would drink again. I had been dry for about three weeks when I went to a Christmas street market with Emily.

There were revellers everywhere, and we passed many of my old haunts that night. I also met several people I had drank with, but none of these distractions put the thought of taking a drink into my head. Emily was looking better, and I think she was beginning to cautiously hope that I was going to make it this time.

I was still a nervous wreck and prone to mood swings, but they were nowhere near as bad as when I'd been drinking. I think she could see that I was really trying, and that A.A. seemed to be helping me in a way nothing else had in the past. My head was clearing and I was making an effort to spend some time with the kids, but I could only manage this for short periods before my patience would run out.

I had never learnt how to be a proper parent, it was a lot more difficult than I imagined. There were no Christmas presents in for the kids. Even in the worst years of my drinking Santa had been good to my kids, and for some strange reason I had always managed to stay dry on Christmas day. There was very little money for presents and I was in a mad panic about this. When I shared this at a meeting people told me not to worry, and do what you can.

A Daddy not drinking is the best present you will ever give them. This did little to assuage my feelings of inadequacy. We had a family meeting in early December and I told the kids there would not be much for Christmas this year, I told them about my drinking problem and how I was getting help with it.

They were too young to understand. I was trying to prepare them for a disappointing Christmas morning the only way I knew how. Big boxes full of cheap rubbish, was all they got that year.

I did manage to make it the Christmas they still remember most vividly to this day. I had a cunning, if somewhat unorthodox plan to make Christmas special, and it took a lot of persuasion to get Emily to go along with it.

Our house had a bay window and the curtains went across the bay, rather than around the inside of it. When the kids charged down the stairs on Christmas morning the curtains were still closed "I'm sorry but Santa didn't come this year" I said.

There was not a present to be seen, shocked into total silence and with tears welling up they were ushered into the kitchen for their breakfast by Emily, who closed the door behind her.

I opened the curtains and took the presents out from their hiding place and shouted into the kitchen "Kids Santa's been".

The best kind of all hell broke loose in our living room that morning. I'm crying as I write this, for it has only just dawned on me, that this was one of the first times that I had ever done something for my kids, simply to make them happy.

There was no sense of "duty or obligation", no "anything for a bit of peace" and most importantly of all, no "what's in it for me" involved.

I have only just realised that A.A. was already changing my attitude. I shared this story at the Christmas meeting, everybody had a good laugh. It made a pleasant change to have people laughing with me instead of at me. We had a great day with no arguments and a relaxed atmosphere in the family home.

That night as I lay in bed with my lovely Emily snuggled up to me I remembered a thought from a long time ago. "Don't go back to the madness you've too much to lose". Even though I could not see it, a gradual change was taking place between my ears. My mind was slowly opening up to the possibility that I could indeed find a way to live at peace with myself.

During the holiday period we visited friends and family, played with the kids, and did all the normal family things. I was still nervous in a social setting, but everyone knew not to offer me alcohol, so there was no pressure and no urge to lift a glass. My family were having a house party on New Year's Eve. I asked a friend in A.A. if it was wise to go, he suggested that it would probably be better if I didn't.

He said that if I was going, make sure your family know that if you felt uncomfortable you would leave. Explain to them that it would be self preservation that would take you away, not a desire to snub them, or be unsociable.

I decided to show my face, but not to stay for long, this would be the first time I had been in a heavy drinking environment, since quitting seven weeks earlier. I went to the party, which was only a short walk from home at about half past ten, reasoning that I would be able have a soft drink, see in the New Year and go home.

Most people were three sheets to wind when I arrived, and I never got to sing "auld lang syne". One drunken reveller kept pestering me about how well I was doing without the drink, when I looked at him, I saw my old self in my final binge.

I was not yet strong enough to look back at this. I excused myself and quietly left and went home. When I entered the house Emily was hot on my heels. I was shaking and nervous, but there was no urge to drink. I snapped at her that I didn't need a baby sitter, and told her to go back to the party. She was close to tears for she thought I was going to hit the bottle.

I apologised and assured her that I was too nervous to stay at the party, just in case the craving would return. I insisted she go back and see in the New Year, but there was no chance of that happening. We saw out the old year together on our own.

I still use the defence of leaving early from social events if people get too drunk. Listening to someone going over the same story ten times, whilst talking like a washing machine, is not my idea of stimulating conversation.

The relief of getting past the festive season, not only with not having taken alcohol, but also not having any desire to do so put me in good spirits and positivity was returning to my thinking. 1990 was going to be a good year and nothing was going to distract me from making up for the way I had been treating my family.

My new found enthusiasm brought cautionary words from my friends in A.A., they did not want to dampen my spirit, but they explained that lots of people had went through a "Honeymoon Period" and then hit the bottle. They urged me to get on the twelve step programme, before something bad brought me down to earth with a bump. I could see that although I had done well in school, I had failed miserably in the "University of Life".

I now look upon A.A. as a classroom in this university, and the wise heads therein are my professors. I will refer to them as this, from here on in. I took their advice and started working on the twelve steps. Within a few weeks I had completed them, and proudly told a professor that I had learnt the steps. He laughed and told me the recovery programme was not like learning your tables at school. "You have to live the steps to understand them". "I do understand them, I can recite them backwards if you want". "You'll probably go backwards as well, if you think you're cured" he said.

I was angry, but this was the man I had once drank with, and had seen such a change in when I first came to the rooms. I trusted him and asked what I should do.

He told me to take them one at a time, and as I came to understand them, try to find a way to apply them to my daily living. I still couldn't understand why this was so important.

He said that since coming to the rooms I had stopped going to the pub, tried to be good to my family and live a decent life, I was doing well, but I had probably only done these things because I was frightened of what might happen if I drank again. That's the reaction of an immature mind to a problem, find a quick fix.

If I wanted long term peace in my head, I needed to completely change my thinking. Arrogance, being self centred, seeking praise to bolster my self-esteem, never thinking about how my actions affected others, jealousy, the list of character defects seemed endless. He told me some of these defects could be removed, others controlled, and some could be turned into assets.

Start by doing things for other people without looking for something in return. He told me that "HOW" stands for honesty, open mindedness and willingness. We say "The Serenity Prayer" at the end of the meetings, he told me to think about its words, and what they meant.

I had a vague notion about what he was trying to share with me, but no real grasp of the concept of the steps. The one asset I did have, was the ability to be honest enough with myself to recognise many of my character defects. This gave me enough material to work on for now. I was under no illusions about my chances of staying off drink. I had been to hell and back too often to think I could beat this on my own.

More and more these days I was involved with family activities. I was at meetings most nights, but before the meetings and at weekends, free time was occupied with home-works, or just playing with the kids. There was another part of married life which I had neglected for too long, and would have to deal with sooner, rather than later.

Our finances were a complete shambles. I had refused to even look at household bills in the last few months of my drinking and there was a cupboard full of unopened envelopes for me to deal with. My professor told me this was all part of being a grown-up, other people dealt with these things without giving it a second thought. Everything was in arrears, how could I ever catch up. I was advised to go and talk to my creditors and make arrangements to pay off what I could afford.

Never having been really involved with family life in the way any normal father should be, and with the added pressure of our dire financial situation, I found it difficult to juggle my new role and also find time for meetings. By now I had acquired a copy of "The Big Book" of A.A., this is like a roadmap to sobriety, some think of it as A.A.'s bible. I read this so that I might better understand the steps.

Finding Sobriety

In finding sobriety I describe how I interpret the Twelve Step Programme of Recovery, and how I have tried to apply it to my life. It seems like a daunting task, and the distractions of everyday life slow progress to a snail's pace at times. In truth when I was in the middle of it with a brain still addled by the effects of my drinking career, I didn't really know what was going on.

I have intertwined some of the experiences of my daily living into my interpretation of the steps, this makes it somewhat disjointed. But that is exactly what my early days in recovery were like as I stumbled along my path to sobriety.

This is why finding a friend you can trust, and whose sobriety you respect is so important for recovery to be successful. I call them my professors from the University of Life, in Alcoholics Anonymous they are normally referred to as Sponsors.

Step 1

** We admitted we were powerless over alcohol,
that our lives had become unmanageable. **

As I've already said I had no problem with the first half of this statement, if I'd disagreed with this I'd still be out there drinking. It was the second part I couldn't get my head around. I needed to figure this bit out but life was distracting me from my studies, progress towards understanding the recovery programme was very slow. But I was starting to grasp the concept of an unmanageable life. It was my emotions that were unmanageable, not the routine things of daily living.

Thinking before reacting made it much easier to deal with life's problems. Reflecting on how I dealt with issues helped me correct mistakes, instead of continuing along the wrong path. Listening to other people's ideas, instead of always believing I knew best, made me realise I was not as clever as I thought I was.

Oddly enough I recognised these concepts, for it was exactly this type of attitude that had made me successful in my work life. Why then could I not carry this over into the emotional side of my life, and what was stopping me from applying the same concepts to life at home.

I came to see that the one area where I had complete confidence in my ability, was golf course maintenance, for having grown up steeped in the job I had no fear in that environment. I discussed this with my professors and they shared their experience with me. They described me as "DRY" because I was not drinking, but they told me sobriety was much more than that.

To achieve sobriety I would have to become as comfortable at home, as I was when I escaped into work, where I felt confident and in control. Making mistakes trying to handle life is normal, but most normal people learnt from their errors, and did better the next time. I realise now that when I was younger, acute self awareness, and an over sensitive nature, stopped me from trying again when I blundered, for I thought it was more important for me not to look stupid, than to stop being stupid.

Mr Nasty was much less frightening now, and only surfaced when I was in a panic about the horrendous state of our finances. Eating large slices of humble pie, I went round all my creditors and apologised for being in arrears. I told them honestly what the problem had been, and made arrangements to pay up the arrears as soon as possible.

Much to my surprise, I received a sympathetic ear from every one of them, one young lady even told me not to overstretch my budget trying to pay back too quickly. I did promise too much to my creditor's, for I forgot to allow for little things like clothes and heating, or the cost of running my car, when I worked out my grand plan to put things right. I was not as good at budgeting as I was at sums.

Learning to manage my life was indeed much more difficult than I had imagined, but at least I was trying. Hard work was needed if I was to ever achieve the peace and contentment I saw in my professors.

I am now convinced that if I hadn't followed through on changing my personality, I would probably have drank again at some stage.

Work was going very well and life at home was steadily getting better, the tension and fear that had been part of Emily's life for so long, was slowly receding and there were smiles for me now, not just for the kids.

Even though things were improving, the fear in me was still there, I didn't feel in control, self-doubt, insecurity and shame about my past still lingered in my head.

The format at most A.A. meetings is that the secretary runs the meeting and one person with a minimum term of sobriety shares their story from the top table before the meeting is opened to the floor.

With my first three months behind me I was eligible to do my first chair. I was looking forward to this privilege for it is a significant milestone in anyone's journey to sobriety, I was a bit nervous but told my drunk story and how I was feeling now.

The sharing back reminded me of my second meeting when people had focussed on me and encouraged me to keep coming back. At the end of the meeting everyone congratulated me on reaching this milestone.

I took up golfing again and became Captain of the green keeper's golfing society. On my captain's day we played a prank on a sales rep who was playing as one of my guests, we switched his golf ball on the first tee and everyone had a great laugh when it exploded in a cloud of white powder when he hit off. The day went well and ended perfectly for me when I had the privilege of presenting my Dad with first prize. He quietly said "the change in you is the only prize I needed".

I had to make a quick exit to the toilets if my colleagues were not to see me cry. My professors had told me things like this would happen, they had said other people would see the change in me long before I would.

Dad's words encouraged me to dig deeper into the "twelve steps" for I wanted more of this good life, and I knew I still needed to work hard to change my thinking and get peace in my head.

Step 2

* Came to believe that a Power greater than our selves could restore us to sanity. *

I had great difficulty with this step because many in A.A. referred to this power as "God". The concept of God, as depicted in organised religions did not sit well with me, when I discussed this with one of my professors he showed me a way to accept this step as being true.

In each one of us there is at least some power for good, if I share my problem one to one with another person, his power will work for me to help find a solution. If I share at a meeting, the collective power of everybody there will multiply this effect. It was very simple, yet until then I could not see, that "A trouble shared, is indeed a trouble halved". The support and love I felt in an A.A. room was, and still is a Power greater than myself.

I was less than a year of booze and the craving for drink still had not returned. Even though I still had a troubled mind, it was a lot better than it had been. I was growing up and dealing with life with much more confidence now. I no longer procrastinated over every little task put in front of me. I was trying to apply my attitude in work to the rest of daily living, and it was starting to work.

I was stumbling and blundering my way to sobriety, making mistakes, getting angry and giving up at some point almost every day. But I now had a power greater than myself, and that, coupled with the memory of my last drunken binge spurred me on to keep trying.

I had heard someone say at a meeting "sit back and watch the miracles happen", one of the old hands told me not to take that too literally. I knew what he meant, for every time I eased up on trying to move on with the programme, I could feel myself slipping back into my old way of thinking. I asked a professor what happens when the "Honeymoon period" comes to an end. He told me to stop worrying about things that might never happen. Live in today, not in your fears. Easier said than done I thought, but his words helped me, and I continued to try to live a decent way of life. This was not because I wanted to be well thought of, it was self preservation, and although I didn't realise at the time, it was the start of making amends to my family. This has given me peace in my head, and I've learnt to like myself.

The "Good Wolf" within was strong now, but his alter ego had not gone away and every once in a while he would claw at my back, trying to get out of his cage.

Keeping to my agreements with my creditors had not been easy, and the lack of money for little extras at home was making me feel inadequate as the bread winner. Guilt about the mess I had gotten us into was eating at me, and constantly reminding me of my wayward past. There was no urge to drink, but when the guilt took hold I had no peace in my head, and was hard to live with.

This came to a head one Friday afternoon, I was going to the bank to pay some bills, and had taken my daughter with me to buy her new trainers. Lisa was only seven years old, she must have thought it strange when I stopped outside the bank and muttered aloud "Fuck it! You bastards are getting nothing more from me".

I turned around and headed to the shoe shop, where I bought everyone in the house new shoes, Lisa got two pairs, for she was due a new pair before we left home. We arrived home and I proudly presented the family with their new shoes. The kids were happy, Emily was not amused "did you pay the bills?" she asked. "I've paid enough it's time we had a treat" I replied, I'd messed up and I knew it, but I was not about to back down. During the blazing row that ensued she laid into me in a way she would never have dared to if I'd been drinking.

Back to sulking like a child, I stormed out of the house and took off in my car. The steering wheel got pounded until my fists were too sore to continue. I parked up and gradually calmed down, Emily was right I could not be trusted to behave responsibly. I had been warned by some of my creditors that there would be no further chances, if I didn't stick to what I'd agreed. Back home with my tail between my legs, I apologised and promised to make things right.

After the meeting that night, I shared this experience one to one with my most trusted professor. I was expecting another rollicking from him, for he didn't miss and hit the wall when he thought I was out of line.

He simply asked if I'd taken a drink because of this, the answer was no. He then said "I want you to be honest with me now, did you think about taking a drink?" again the answer was an honest no. He told me not to worry about it, and suggested I go back to the relevant creditors and make new arrangements that allowed me to live within my means. He told me that it's not the mistakes that matter, it's how we react to them. He said I had passed a big test that day, for I had completely lost control, but had not thought of taking a drink.

He also said that I must be doing something right at home, because Emily was no longer frightened of me, and would probably not let me off the hook, if I messed up again. He left me with one final suggestion: If your heads full of crap, get it out, and keep getting it out, until it stays out. At the start of that day my head had been like a pressure cooker, I had allowed a series of small problems to fester in me to the point where I exploded.

I left the meeting with peace in my head, determined to keep working at this new way of life. I went in person to my creditors and explained what had happened, they accepted my apologies and allowed me to make new, more realistic arrangements to clear my debts. The new longer terms were more expensive, but that was a price I was prepared to pay to relieve the pressure on our budget. It took me ten years to clear up the financial mess, and get a decent credit rating.

Step 3

Made a decision to turn our will and our lives over to the care of God as we understood him.

Even today I am still no further on with the concept of God as some sort of unseen entity, which is guiding us through life. I don't knock this idea, but having put my faith in A.A. and never having been let down. I do not feel the need to search for anything else.

My God as I understand him, is still the collective support I get, not just in A.A. for I now have the love of my family to back this up. Perhaps there is a God working through these people. I don't know and frankly I don't care. What I have seems to work for me.

Turning my will and my life over to the care of my God on a daily basis, is still the most difficult thing for me to do consistently. This involves putting complete trust in others, and allowing life to evolve, rather than running around like a headless chicken, thinking I can always make things happen in a way that suits me. Of course I have to make decisions regarding my work, and I have to take certain actions to achieve things in life. But it is actions and decisions that have an adverse effect on others that I must avoid.

Trying to run other people's lives to achieve the outcome I want, with no regard for other people's feelings or point of view, is one of the things that drove me to madness in the first place.

I believe that the first two steps are about accepting my alcoholism, and finding the belief that things can get better. Once that faith has been established, these steps only need to be re-visited in times of doubt.

Step three must be lived on a daily basis to keep that doubt at bay, and allow me to have peace in my head. We end every A.A. meeting with a prayer, I look upon this as the shorthand version of the steps, and I use it every day to help me keep my feet firmly on the ground, whilst getting on with life.

The Serenity Prayer

God grant me the Serenity.

To accept the things I cannot change.

Courage to change the things I can.

And the Wisdom to know the difference.

When I manage to take a back seat, and stop trying to manipulate everything to the way I want it to be. When I stop trying to bend people to my will, I have a good day.

Needless to say, I had plenty of bad days in my early attempts at true sobriety, it is very difficult to break the habits of a lifetime. I still have bad times, but they are few and far between, and rarely last a full day.

Life was good now, I had learnt a lot in my first two years in Alcoholics Anonymous, and was very grateful for the gift of sobriety. I regularly did my turn as secretary, and went round lots of other meetings. I had attended between five and seven meetings each week during those first two years. The whole purpose of A.A. is to try to return suffering alcoholics to a normal way of life, and I felt strong enough in my sobriety to reduce the number of meetings, so that I could spend more time with my family.

Emily was no longer the gaunt, frightened, miserable individual I had created in my drunken madness, and the kids didn't have to walk on egg shells when I was at home. We had our problems and our disputes like any other family, but there was a warm and happy atmosphere in our home, and plenty of laughter and leg pulling went on. I reckoned that if things never got any better, this would do for me. I had escaped the madness, and all I had to do was keep working on the steps, and going to meetings to reinforce my sobriety.

Step 4

Made a searching and fearless moral inventory of ourselves.

My professor explained this step as facing up to my shortcomings and character defects, so that I would have a more honest view of what I was really like.

I wrote down all the bad things I had done, and all the trouble I had caused. This was a struggle back then, for it is not easy to look into your soul, and lay bare the pain from your past.

Having compiled my list of misdemeanours, I showed it to my professor, he read it and scrunched it up into a ball. He told me if this was all I had to say, then I truly was the evil bastard I had once believed myself to be.

He explained that I had misunderstood what was meant by a moral inventory, and said that I should have two columns, every time I wrote something bad, I should try to find some good in me, to balance the books.

"When you did something bad in drink, did you feel guilty when you sobered up"? He asked, "All the time" I replied "Did you do the same bad things when you were sober"? "No way" I said.

"That is the good in you, your conscience beat you into the ground, and forced you into these rooms looking for help" He gave me the little ball of paper and told me to go home and start again.

"Don't beat yourself up for being human, look honestly at the good and the bad" was his parting suggestion. In doing as suggested some of my self esteem was restored for I did indeed find some good in me during this process.

We acquired a dog at home not long after I quit drinking, and we all loved it dearly, one of the kids opened the door for me when I came home from work one evening, the dog bolted out the door and ran under my car, and into the road beyond. The passing driver had no chance to stop, and "Cuddles" was killed. The driver was the father of Alexander's best friend, he was in as bad a state as the rest of us.

In times past I would have hated him for what he'd done, but I really was different now, and we comforted each other, and the kids as best we could. We took "Cuddles" to my work the next morning, and buried him in the woods. The kids made a cross for his grave and always visited him when they came to work with me.

Shortly after this, Edward was riding on a mini-motorbike in the school playground one evening. He went headlong into an iron gate, and was badly cut on the face. My neighbour brought him home, for he was frightened to come home by himself, in case he was in trouble. I did not fly off the handle, and took Edward to A&E, where he was treated for his injuries, which thankfully were not to serious. I did chastise him when we returned home, but not too harshly, for he was sore and I think he had learnt his lesson.

Lisa was struck down with whooping cough and had to stay in the fever hospital. This was just a short distance from my work, and I was able to visit her during the day. It was frightening to watch her cough so violently and persistently, that she often struggled for breath. But I comforted her and she gradually got better. Finally I was growing up, my thinking and reactions had been radically changed, and one day at a time I was coping with whatever life threw at me in a mature, and sensible way, just like most normal people did.

Step 5

Admitted to God, to ourselves, and to another human being the exact nature of our wrongs.

Having completed my revised moral inventory, I once again showed it to my professor, the skeletons were out of the closet. He read it, and once and again scrunched it up into a ball. He shared some of his worst escapades from his drinking career, and told me I was not that different from most people in the rooms. I was not alone in the way I had felt or reacted, but it was not the right way to behave.

When I took that first drink I was unable to control my actions, and therefore was not responsible for my behaviour. This sounded like a Kop-out to me and I said so, he told me it was in some people's eyes, but the only real Kop-out was if I didn't try to do better in future. Staying away from drink, and doing right by the people I cared for would give me peace in my head.

I had no excuses now, and my conscience would destroy me if I went back to my old ways. Curiosity got the better of me, and I asked why he'd scrunched up my list, he told me that's just my way of putting your shame and guilt in the dustbin, and suggested I should do the same.

Somehow seeing my past in print, coupled with our sharing, did help me to get rid of my shame and guilt. I will always have my regrets about my past, but I can't turn back the clock. Today I live with peace in my head, content in the knowledge that I have done everything I can, to make amends to those I hurt.

Step 6

Were entirely ready to have God remove these defects of character.

I still have no faith in the concept of God, as depicted by the organised religions. I have nothing against people who worship together in churches, I simply have a different type of faith.

I found a God of my own understanding, and accept it as my higher power. I have no issues with using this to help me remove my defects.

I have already defined this as the support, and unconditional love I receive from my family, and the members of A.A.

Whatever way I choose to define "My God" is nobody else's business. If it helps to give me confidence and a positive outlook, there's a good chance it will also help me to stay sober. This has been my experience, and it has not let me down during more than 22 years of sobriety. May you be as comfortable with your "God" as I am with mine.

Step 7

Humbly asked him to remove our shortcomings.

Having worked hard on my sobriety, and not been too proud to seek advice from the professors. I now had a reasonable knowledge of the defects I suffered from, which are well enough described in my drunk story.

I was also aware of which ones most often gave me trouble. For me it is the thoroughness applied to the first five steps, that makes it easy to let go of my defects and shortcomings.

But it only works one day at a time, for I do not believe they will ever leave me completely. I am a fallible human being, and if I ever fool myself into believing that I have no defects, the next thought is likely to be that I'm cured, and can drink again.

This is the power of alcohol, I have seen it too many times in fellow sufferers, who think they can give it one more try, and end up dead or insane.

So I start each day by reminding myself how far I've come from the madness, and think about the serenity prayer. This helps me to keep the "Bad Wolf" within locked in his cage.

Step 8

Made a list of all persons we had harmed, and became willing to make amends to them all.

In my drunken years I was blinded to the harm I was doing by a self centred attitude. How could I see beyond my own needs, if I never bothered to look.

Thankfully my list was not overly long, for it was almost always the same small group who suffered when I drank. Top of the list was my wife and children, closely followed by my family.

It took quite a long time before I felt strong enough to open my catalogue of misdemeanours, and start to put things right. But I have done so to the best of my ability, and no longer have to cross the street, when I see people I know coming towards me.

Step 9

Made direct amends to such people wherever possible, except when to do so would injure them or others.

I will never forget the outpouring of love and forgiveness I received, when I apologised to my family and friends for my past behaviour. By the time I was confident enough to believe I was not going to go back to my old ways, they could all see the change in me. Not one person cast doubt on my sincerity or commitment. Their forgiveness helped remove my guilt and shame.

There are people I have not made amends to, but if the opportunity arises I will do so, provided the amends will not cause them more pain.

Sometimes it is best not to disturb their blissful ignorance, so rather than doing further damage just to ease my conscience. I must leave some things unresolved, thankfully there are no major misdeeds left in the closet.

Step 10

Continued to take personal inventory and when we were wrong promptly admitted it.

This step is self explanatory, and is what stops me from letting things fester within until there is no peace in my head. When I fail to carry through with this step in my daily life, it is not long before my conscience starts to give me a hard time.

So I reflect on my actions, even as I'm doing them, to make sure I am not taking away anybody else's peace, or harming anyone.

When I look back on my day, and find I've done something wrong. I can sleep soundly in the knowledge, that I will try to rectify my error at the earliest opportunity, and apologise where necessary.

This moral code has not made me a saint, for I fail at it every day. I'm nobody's doormat, and admitting I'm wrong doesn't come naturally, but I get peace in my head when I manage apply step 10 to my life.

Step 11

Sought through prayer and meditation to improve our conscious contact with God as we understood Him, praying only for knowledge of his will for us and the power to carry that out.

I have my serenity prayer, and sharing with my professors gives me a deeper understanding of the need to not let my will dominate my thought processes.

When I'm at work I spend a lot of time driving between my customers. I have developed the ability to relax on these journeys, and take stock of my assets. Rather than constantly deride myself for my shortcomings as I once did.

I now know that learning to like myself generates positive thinking, and helps keep the "Bad Wolf" within locked in his cage.

I must not return to manipulating and conniving to make things go my way. I must make my decisions in life based on doing what is for the common good of those close to me.

I must accept the outcome of any situation, to be what was meant to happen, whether I like it or not. If I start to think it is me who is in control of my recovery, my ego will soar.

I will be in danger of forgetting that my way always led to trouble and madness. No matter how long I am away from booze it is still only an arm's length away on a bad day, if I abandon what the steps and A.A. has taught me.

Step 12

Having had a spiritual awakening as the result of these steps, we tried to carry this message to other alcoholics, and to practice these principles in all our affairs.

I don't pretend to understand the phrase "Spiritual awakening", but I know that my new way of life has given me freedom from the fangs of alcoholism. (Fear, Arrogance, Negativity, Guilt, Selfishness) I still have all these defects and many more, but they no longer dominate my thinking. I am not responsible for this change, something intangible is working on my behalf.

They say in A.A. that we must give our gift away to keep it, so I must give freely to help others. This is one of the best ways to protect my sobriety. In doing so I am given constant reminders of where I have come from, and there is no better feeling than to know I have helped a fellow sufferer.

The steps are my road map for living with peace in my head, they work when I try to live by the principles of this simple programme of recovery. I see no sense in tempting disaster by abandoning them, and going back to trying to run things my way.

Another "pearl of Wisdom" often heard in A.A. is that To repeat the same mistake twice is stupidity, to keep on making the same mistake over and over again, and expect a different outcome is insanity. Been there, done that, paid a big price for the T-shirt. No thanks!

All Grown Up

We had been married almost sixteen years, and I was in my third year off booze before we went on our first proper family holiday, a week in a caravan at the beach, eight miles from home. My ego would tell me this wasn't much of a holiday, we should be going to Spain, common sense said be grateful for what you have.

The kids loved it and so did we, by the middle of the week I could feel the stress of the pressures of life lifting. I hadn't even realised I was under stress, I resolved to make sure we got away every year if we could afford it, for I realised that it doesn't matter where you go, a break from the norm is a good way to re-charge the batteries.

It was during this holiday that we almost lost our oldest son, Alex was playing with his new inflatable dingy when we left him to go make dinner. Shortly after we returned to the caravan, one of our neighbours came up shouting frantically that our son was in trouble

We rushed to the beach to find him blue with the cold, and shivering uncontrollably. Back at the caravan we wrapped him in blankets, and did what we could to get some heat into him. When he recovered I asked what had happened.

He had lent his dingy to two young girls, who lost the paddles and drifted out to sea. Not yet fourteen years old, he had swam out and towed them back to shore. I told Alex it was very brave to save the girls, but always get the help of an adult in future.

He said "I didn't do it for the stupid girls, I wanted my boat back". "A chip off the old block" I thought, but this was not true, for I would have milked it, I would have revelled in being the hero.

A new golf course was to be built not far from home. I applied for the job of growing it in, and was successful. It was goodbye to the staff who had saved my career.

I wrote a letter to my boss explaining that I would never leave this job simply to move to another course, it was only the chance to build a course from scratch that had lured me away. A cynic reading the letter may have thought I was making sure I did not burn my bridges.

This was not the case, for my sentiments were genuine, and I had too much respect for my boss to ever consider trying to manipulate him. I also spoke to him personally, and thanked him for his help with my drinking problem.

My new job came with a tied cottage, we were now living out in the country and I only had to cross the road to be on the golf course.

Emily gave up her job and went to work in a hotel adjacent to the new golf course, so there were big changes all round.

Fortunately we were still in the same school district, this meant that the kid's education would not be disrupted. There were no buses apart from the school run, "Dads Taxi" was constantly in demand for Mum didn't drive.

Alex was into running and thought nothing of trekking the three miles cross country to see his mates. He would return through the pitch black forest at the end of the day. Edward and the twins had regular sleepover guests, and life was very good in this tranquil country setting.

Building a golf course involves long hours, sometimes seven days a week, but I thrived in this environment and got a real buzz out of dealing with the very different aspects of this new challenge. It was not like the routine course maintenance I was Familiar with, there were endless meetings with contractors, planners, and of course the owners. Snap decisions had to be made to keep the project on schedule.

This was not an issue, for I was confident in my ability, and I knew that most of the decisions would be made jointly with my deputy, the architect, and the contractors.

My kid's had a ball playing on the site, a 247acre back garden is not something to be sneezed at. They were never away from the diggers, and could often be seen driving a quad around the course.

There was a path through some trees, which divided into two to go round a large tree. David was riding a quad with his twin sister on the back, as he drove along this path he could not make up his mind which path to take. So he decided not to decide, the quad tried to climb the tree and the twins were pitched off, with poor Lisa ending up in the nettles beside the path.

Pride was the only real casualty, but Lisa was teased by her brothers about all the bright red blotches on her fair skin. I remembered how I had reacted when I was teased as a kid, and was happy to see that she could give as good as she got and then forget about it.

My antics as a drunk did not appear to have had an adverse effect on the kids. They were all far better at getting on with life than I ever was.

It was humbling to realise that my kids were as mature now, as I had been in my mid-thirties.

Emily loved our new home, it didn't matter that she couldn't drive, she was happy to walk the short distance to work. She often went for long walks with her sister, on the country estate the golf course was part of.

I continued to attend A.A. regularly and now found life very rewarding. Another very rewarding aspect from this time was the freedom I was given to run the golf course, I got to design the interior of the maintenance shed, select my own equipment, work up my budgets and produce my own maintenance programme.

The only member of my crew I was not permitted to select was my deputy course manager. This was because my brother had applied for the post.

He was successful, he was also the only other person on the team with experience in golf course maintenance, for I wanted no bad habits brought in from other courses.

I was even allowed to write the staff employment contracts. It would be two years before the course would be open, plenty of time to train the rookies.

Having given me complete control over the "Grow-In", the owners turned up the heat when bad weather forced a halt to the work. Back to back very wet years, saw things slow to a crawl at times. Fortunately one of the Directors was a Farmer, and he knew that to work the land in wet conditions would destroy the structure of the soil, but we managed to claw back some of the time. The new course, opened four months behind schedule.

None of the pressure or setbacks made me consider lifting a bottle, for I was practicing the principles of the steps, and taking things one day at a time. Whilst sharing one to one, in the way I was helped when I'd first came around, a troubled young man, not long around the meetings could not see the good things he had in his life.

In frustration he said "It's alright for you, you're happy with your lot". I could not help but smile as I replied" No I'm not happy with my lot, but I've accepted it" Upon reflection, I realised that three important things had come from this conversation.

Firstly, it was good that another human being could see the peace that I had. I also recognised the importance of acceptance as one of the major keys to long term sobriety.

It also demonstrated the fact that even someone new to the fellowship of Alcoholics Anonymous, could have a profound effect on me. His throw-away comment, born out of frustration, had reinforced my sobriety.

Alex started work as an assistant gardener on the country estate, the rest of the kids were now in secondary education and working on the golf course in their spare time, as I had done in my childhood.

Everything was right with the world, and we were booked in to "Butlins" holiday camp in Ayr for a well earned, week long break. Lisa wanted to take her best friend Amy with her for female company.

I didn't object to this, but I was a little worried that Amy's parents might have second thoughts. They had known me when I was drinking, and I couldn't blame them if they were a little nervous about me taking care of their child. My fears were groundless, for they had also witnessed my recovery. Taking the car on the ferry to Stranraer would be followed by an hour long drive to the camp. The excitement was fantastic on the boat, Edward kept pestering us to come and see this, or can I have money for that.

Halfway across and unable to take any more of Edward's enthusiasm, I told him there was a pool table on the ship. He spent much of the rest of the voyage searching for this, without catching on that you couldn't play pool on the rolling sea. We still keep him going about this even today.

Leaving the ferry behind, we made our way to the holiday camp, we were allocated our caravan and the kids disappeared to explore the funfair and other attractions on site. Unlimited use of the subtropical water-world, the funfair rides, and lots of other things were included in the price. The kids had a great time and so did we.

There was very good entertainment laid on in the evenings, this was the first time in my sobriety that I was going to put myself in a drinking environment every night for a week. It would not be fair on Emily for me to sit in the caravan every night and make her miss the shows, for she would not have went without me.

I had been around drink at plenty of family gatherings, and in the early days of my abstinence Emily would not have liquor in the house, I had moved on from then, and she was not a heavy drinker. I had no right to deprive her of the odd glass if she felt like it.

I even went to the off-licence to buy her chosen poison, with no thought of getting some for me. I was quietly confident that I would be alright.

The kids went with us to the shows and we had a great time, not once did I even consider the idea of taking alcohol. I had the address and phone number of A.A. in Ayr with me, just in case I felt the need for a meeting, or just someone to talk to. One of the great things about A.A. is that no matter where you are in the world, you're rarely far from a meeting, and help is only a phone call away.

They say in A.A. that if you keep going to the barber's you'll get your hair cut, so you won't find me in pubs or clubs, except on family occasions, or for a meal.

Despite having spared no expense to give the kids a great holiday, one of their fondest memories of "Butlins" was pushing each other around the camp in the big "wheely bins" used for the laundry, for this got them a chase from the camp security guards. Lisa tried horse riding on the beach while we were there and liked it so much that she wanted lessons when we got home, she still loves to ride, and even managed to get her parents on horseback on our last visit.

We returned to this venue another three times, before our last trip there I suggested a trip to Spain instead and was greeted with a chorus of "What's wrong with Butlins!" Democracy won the day.

Teenage angst was upon us and I did not realise how much my own youthful escapades, and the things I had learnt in A.A. would help my kids through these difficult years. Alex was in the young famer's club, and had fallen in love. His new girlfriend visited occasionally and we liked her and got on well. We didn't see much of him nowadays, he was always out with his girl.

She got a place in a university in Scotland, after she left he did not know what to do with himself for he was missing her terribly. Not long afterwards he got the "Dear John" treatment, she had found someone else. I knew what this felt like and was determined to help him get through his pain. He was heartbroken and angry, for he had treated her well, he could not understand what he saw as betrayal. Self doubt and negativity oozed from every pore. Alone in the car with him I told him he would never forget his first love, although he couldn't see it now, things would get better and time would heal his wounds.

I shared my experience with Shirley all those years ago, I told him it was vital that he did not allow this experience to colour his judgement, and make him withdraw into a shell as I had done. His lost love was not a bad person, they simply weren't meant to be together and it was better to find out now, before the bonds grew stronger.

I knew that no amount of "pearls of wisdom" would help him, but sharing experiences does not just work for alcoholics. Everybody needs reminded that they are not alone in times of trouble.

He slowly got over his loss, and decided to join the navy the following year. I suppose its "better than the foreign legion" I thought, but no he was not running away, he had realised there was no great future in being a gardener, and wanted to find a new challenge in life. With renewed positivity he prepared for enlistment. He was already fit, but he had made enquiries about what was ahead of him, and knew the initial training would be tough. He put himself through a punishing fitness programme to make things easier at training camp.

Around this time serious political unrest was creating havoc in the estate where most of Emily's family lived.

We suggested they come to our house for bonfire night on the 11th of July, to get them out of the area, in case there was trouble. We ended up with a couple of tents in the garden, as well as a house full of guests. I didn't drink, but I had my Dad's old recipe for punch, and made and about five gallons of the stuff. The party lasted for three days. These "Alternative Bonfire Nights" became an annual event for about four years, with more and more people turning up each time.

It was ironic that someone who was allergic to drink, and looked upon it as a poison, was dubbed the hero of the hour. My punch was now considered legendary by the revellers. Lisa and her cousin even managed to get drunk on the non-alcoholic version I made for myself.

David was the most laid back of my kids, but not so when the barbeque was on the go at the parties, he was the self appointed head chef. I think he ate almost as much as he cooked, but he did become quite accomplished with the tongs and charcoal, and has since become a very good cook.

The parties were getting beyond control. I called a halt to them when I found a total stranger wandering around our bedrooms in a drunken stupor.

I used the excuse that the trouble had subsided in the estate. It was about time somebody else took a turn at hosting one of these nights. The parties are still remembered with fondness by all those who took part. I still attended A.A. meetings, though not as regularly as I once had, but the recovery programme was always with me, for I knew better than to stray from its path.

Edward had always been the rascal of the bunch, always up to mischief, always showing off. I still have a picture of him as a two year old, dressed in a bright red sleep-suit with yellow vinyl feet, sitting in the bathroom sink with his feet in the air, and a silly "Look at Me" smile, pasted from ear to ear. Thank goodness the camera was handy that day.

He had a wicked sense of humour, and although very small for his age this never seemed to bother him. He had lots of friends and seemed very happy most of the time. He decided he wanted to become an architect, for he loved technical drawing and was very creative.

He started his further education in architecture at the local technical college. The equipment he needed was very expensive, but we supported him in his new venture, happy that he had positive goals in his head.

This didn't last long, for the early part of the training involved a lot of heavy going learning the history of architecture. Edward could not hack this dull and boring work and was very unhappy, he wanted to find a job and leave the tech. He got a job with a firm which supplied machinery to me at work. He sold all the expensive equipment I had supplied, of course it was his now, so Dad saw none of the money.

He was soon to come down to earth, for in his new job he was very much the junior hand, and was rightly treated as such. A cheeky smile and a quick wit only get you so far in the world of work. Edward's confidence was disappearing, and his sensitive side was making him moody, and hard to live with.

He snapped at everyone, and the heated arguments with his younger siblings over the slightest thing were frequent. The guy who was always saying "Live life it's not a rehearsal" had completely vanished from our home.

This could not go on and I had a quiet word with some of his work colleagues, whom I'd known for years. They told me they liked him, but sometimes he was far too full of himself, and would have to be reminded of his place in the pecking order at work.

Although he is now taller than me, he had not yet sprouted up, and their perception of him was that he was just a little kid. I knew this was wrong and Edward would resent this, but I also knew he had to learn to live with it for the time being. He could only change their perception of him by earning their respect. I knew he would do this given time, but he had to drop the "know it all" attitude, and get back to being himself.

I didn't know what to do about this, but I had to try something. A few home truths might help, after picking him up from work one evening, I broached the subject of the serious change in his attitude and got a surly shrug of the shoulders as an answer.

He couldn't get out of the moving car, I would have my say. I tried to be tactful about the transition into the world of work, and how he needed to fit in, and respect his colleagues. He didn't seem to be listening, but I continued trying to give advice that I thought might help him.

There was still no response, not even an argument. It was as if this was going in one ear, and out the other. Enough of this crap I thought, I never raised my voice, but I gave him both barrels.

I told him he could carry on whatever way he wanted to at work, but the attitude at home had to change, none of us were going to take any more shit from him. I then said that for someone who used to always say "Live life, it's not a rehearsal" he wasn't even turning up for rehearsals.

Something must have struck a nerve, for he was sitting crying in the car. I didn't know if I'd handle this well or not, but I knew from my own experience, that letting things build up inside did nobody any good. I was worried that if he continued on his present path, he could be heading for a heap of trouble, if nothing else I had given Edward food for thought. He did come round, and the real Edward we knew and loved soon returned to his wicked best. He got on well in his job, but left after a few years for pastures new.

He has recently returned to the firm where he first started work, now he is part of the management team. I'll keep my little ego trip, and believe that something I said back then helped him.

The Good Years

Lisa was working in a chip shop at nights, and often didn't get home until the early hours. I was awakened from a deep sleep by the sound of a loud bang. I could see nothing when I looked from my window into the darkness of the winter's night.

I was about to get back into bed thinking I had been dreaming, when I heard a siren and saw blue lights flashing. I ran downstairs to find Lisa crying in the front garden. As she was about to exit her taxi a speeding car with no lights had taken the door out of her hand, another two seconds it would have taken her as well.

The drunk driver had then crashed through the hedge on the other side of the road, and was being treated by paramedics. A chill ran through me when I thought of what might have happened to my daughter. An even colder chill hit me later when I realised how lucky I'd been not to kill someone with my car when I'd been drinking.

I will always be grateful that no such event occurred during my hundreds of drunken driving episodes, but everybody drove with drink taken back then. Thank goodness they didn't all drink like me, it would have led to carnage on the roads if they had.

Alex had completed his basic training in the royal navy, so off we went to Plymouth for his passing out parade, we were so proud, as of course all the parents were that day. We met some of his instructors, and were given an appraisal of his progress. All the trainees were given nicknames, his was "Tackleberry" after the character from the "Police Academy" films. Very appropriate, for he always gives his fanatical best at whatever he tackles.

Emily was so embarrassed when we went into Plymouth the next day for a stroll around town, Alex could not stop himself from marching along, ramrod straight, and arms swinging as if he were still on the parade ground. We had a great weekend, and it was good to see Alex happy and doing so well. His instructor told us that he only lost the top recruit cup in the final week of his training, and predicted a successful career for him in the navy.

The other three kids had made the most of us being away for the passing out parade. Upon returning home the tell tale signs of party-time were obvious. There was no serious damage done, and no major complaints from the neighbours.

Emily and I said nothing and were pleased that we could trust them to at least be discreet when left unsupervised for a whole weekend.

This would certainly not have been the case when I was a young teenager, and I was grateful that they were showing far more restraint and common sense than I ever did at that age.

Edward was now in love and the guy who had laughed, as he told us that he would never be tied down, was destined to be the first of my sons to fall of the perch of bachelorhood. When the twins found out he was going steady, they were merciless in their teasing. "These women are devious creatures, you chase them, but they catch you". I teasingly asked him if this might be "the one", and it was obvious that he was as "twitterpated as Bambi" when he said "She's amazing Dad". When he brought Emma home to meet us the teasing ended, and she was looked upon as one of the clan from then on.

Emma is a really nice girl, but also a "very proper young lady". We were not completely unsophisticated, but were much more relaxed in public than she was. Emily suggested we treat the starry eyed pair to a meal in a very good Chinese restaurant.

The night was going well, but degenerated into chaos, when the waiter pronounced the name of Emily's dessert in a funny way and she took a fit of unstoppable giggles.

Emma looked as if she wanted to crawl under the table and hide, for every time the giggles subsided, I would mimic the waiter, and off Emily went again. Before long half the diners were laughing with us, including the waiter, Emma relaxed, she had no choice.

They say in A.A. that if you want to know about the quality of someone's sobriety, you should ask their partner. I must have been doing alright, for Emily was always happy nowadays. Alex returned home on leave, and his stories of life in the senior service made it obvious that he had chosen well with his new career, and was enjoying life to the full.

Lisa was so impressed that she decided to follow in her brothers footsteps, and promptly announced that she was going to enlist in the navy. We thought at first that she just had her head turned by the novelty of seeing her big brother resplendent in his uniform, and listening to the tall tales he told of life at sea, and the escapades they got up to on leave.

We couldn't have been more wrong, and she sent away for her application forms shortly after Alex returned to his ship. We were apprehensive about Lisa's plans, but my daughter is a very determined young woman, and was no different back then.

"Daddy dear, I need your permission to join up" were the dreaded words that put my mind in turmoil. A father's attitude towards his only daughter, is different to that towards his sons. But I realised that I had to let here follow her chosen path in life, without interference bred from illogical prejudice. With much trepidation I signed the forms, and her new adventure began. As we had done for Alex, we had a big send-off party for Lisa, and off she went to Plymouth for basic training.

What I'd learned in A.A. was a great help in overcoming my concerns about Lisa flying the nest so young, for I realised that all the worst scenarios I could imagine, were in fact just my way of trying to hold on to her for my own selfish reasons. I gave her my support, and let her go with a smile to hide my fears. In truth, getting away from the insular nature of life in a small community was one of the best decisions both Lisa and Alex made, and they both benefited from the experiences they had in the navy.

David was the son I was most concerned about during his teenage years. He was always in work, but could not find a job that he was happy in. All my kids took a drink and I made no attempt to stop them, for I knew that would make them rebel, and be counterproductive.

My fear was that if David did not find some meaningful direction in life, he might turn out like me. Despite my A.A. teaching I found it very difficult to rid myself of these fears, for he drank like me, and seemed very unhappy when he was drunk. He started going steady with a lovely young girl called Anne, but still did not seem happy with life.

Thinking I could change things for the better, I blundered in and suggested that he should join the navy. I used all my old manipulative skills to put pressure on him to do what I was suggesting, and he was close to doing it. David did not want to disappoint me, but thankfully his older brother put me in my place. Edward told me that David was in love with Anne, and feared he would lose her if he left to join the navy. I hadn't realised how strong his feelings were for Anne, and if I'd succeeded it would probably have destroyed his future.

So much for live and let live, had I learnt nothing from the madness of my past. I was trying to run things my way, and had come very close to alienating my son, and wrecking his life. I told David to forget about what I wanted, and do what he believed was right for him, He and Anne are now happily married.

I'm glad Edward made me mind my own business. It's easy to talk about the steps, the trouble is life sometimes gets in the way.

Lisa was posted to Scotland after basic training, we visited her there and she seemed very happy with her new career, and had made lots of new friends since enlisting. We enjoyed the visit and went home reassured about her future by the way she was coping in her new environment.

Shortly after returning home Alex phoned to say he was thinking of applying to become a submariner. I told him he'd need to remember to close the doors more than he had at home if he went into subs. His new post would also mean he would be based in the same place as Lisa. Scotland became our holiday home for the next few years, and we enjoyed many great times with our "matlow" offspring in that beautiful country.

Not least, our daughter's wedding, in a little church on the shores of Loch Lomond. Wedding bells were to ring for others long before that occasion. But a time for grieving would precede these happy events, for great sadness was soon to enter Emily's life.

Unknown to us her mother was gravely ill. A phone call from my Mum in law's best friend in England, told us that she had fallen down the stairs and was in severe pain. Emily and her sister went across to help her out for a few days. Emily was crying when she phoned me the next night to say that her Mum was dying, the doctors gave her no more than a week if even that.

We were all in shock, for we had seen her only a few months previous, and there had been not the slightest hint that anything was wrong. I booked my beat up old car onto the ferry, and gathered up Emily's siblings, to take them to see their Mum. We were in the queue for the boat to Fleetwood, but it had engine trouble. We were told to get round to the other ferry terminal, and were taken to Scotland instead of England. It was a race against time from the start, and this didn't help, all I could think about was the poor sister's on their own, watching their mother die, for it had taken two days to organise our trip.

I was also concerned that my ten year old banger might not be up to the long drive down with five adults aboard. The serenity prayer was well worn out by the time we reached our destination. It was the loneliest I had been since I'd put the cork in the bottle.

What can you say to four people in these circumstances, hardly a word was spoken during the five hour drive to the hospital. We arrived shortly after lunchtime, Emily's Mum passed away in the early hours of the following morning, everyone was devastated. I was no longer bereft of emotions, the way I had been when I was a drunk.

I broke down in tears upon seeing the grief stricken family, but I was grateful that we had managed to get there before her passing. This was to be one of the toughest weeks of my life, Emily and her siblings were grieving, but they had none of their extended family there for support during the first couple of days.

The friend from England was the rock we clung to, and she was a great help for us. Her local knowledge guided us to undertakers, where to get death certificates, and all the other duties we needed to perform.

The cremation took place a week later, and thankfully many of the extended family made it over to pay their respects. This had been a very emotional, and challenging week, I thought about drink, but had no urge to take it, I knew this was not an option, and steered clear of any environment where I might have been tempted to drown my sorrows. Other people's feelings dominated my thoughts and actions.

Emily's Mum had family on both sides of the Irish Sea, and it was her wish that her ashes be scattered in the sea, between the two sides of her family. Having friends in the boating community, it was not difficult to arrange this event. Emily and her siblings performed her last request a few weeks after her passing, and regularly go down to the shore, and sit on the rocks to feel close to their Mum.

Edward and Emma set up home together and seemed to be very happy, they did want to get married, but decided to save for a while before tying the knot. We left them to get on with it and were very pleased when, after nearly four years together, they had their big day. Emily and I were delighted, and everything was set in motion for what was our first family wedding.

It was to take place in the same church as my parents had been married in, during world war two.

The run-up to the wedding was a hectic time, but the kids worked through all the arrangements. We made suggestions along the way, and paid our share, but this was their day and we were happy to go along with what they wanted.

Emma asked our daughter to be a bridesmaid along with her sister, and they mixed the two families together when seating them at the reception. These little touches made for a more inclusive experience, and helped make the day a great success.

The happy couple were beautiful, and it brought back memories of my own wedding. I arranged for my wine to be replaced with sparkling apple juice for the toasts, and after the speeches we partied the night away.

Another test passed I thought to myself, for I had not been tempted to take alcohol, in spite of the many offers from guests who were not aware of my condition. Life can be good, and the memories of my children's wedding days are amongst those I cherish most of all.

Soon after this happy occasion Alex phoned to say that he had a new love in his life, her name was Marie, and he would be bringing her home to meet us soon. He asked if I could pick them up from the airport, and I was happy to do so, it was only then that he happened to mention it would be Dublin airport.

The extra hundred miles made no difference, on the day they came home Emily and I set off a good two hours before we needed to, planning to stop for lunch near the airport, before we picked them up. An accident somewhere up ahead of us on the motorway led to us sitting in a traffic jam for ninety minutes.

Lunch turned into a snack at the airport, but we did get there on time to meet Alex, and the girl who was destined to become his wife. Marie was a teacher, who had been training in London, but came from Belfast. Another lovely girl, all my kids are blessed with great life partners, and I think of them as part of the clan.

Lisa was now going strong with a navy man, and I asked Alex if he knew him. He put my mind at ease when he told me her new boyfriend, Richard was a decent bloke, who treated Lisa well.

His approval was good enough for me, for I knew that he would never allow anyone to mistreat his sister, and it was obvious he was comfortable with her choice.

On our next trip to Scotland we met Richard, and even though I couldn't understand his broad Lancastrian accent, and still can't, it was plain to see that he was head over heels with Lisa, and she likewise with him. The naval base had its own ten pin bowling alley, and any nervousness about meeting Lisa's parents soon dissipated when Emily gave us all a laugh as she failed to let go when bowling, and proceeded to follow the bowling ball down the rink on her rear end.

I knew Alex was serious about Marie when he told me he was going to leave the navy to get married. I had learnt my lesson with David and only said "just make sure you're certain before you burn your bridges". He told me eighty five percent of relationships with submariners failed, because not only were you absent for long periods, but there was no way of even knowing where you were, and no contact whatsoever from beneath the waves. He'd made his decision and it was not long before wedding bells were ringing again and another great day was had, when Alex and Marie were married.

Even though it was a March wedding, we were blessed with a bright sunny day, the only thing brighter than the sunshine, was the happy couple's smiles as they enjoyed their day to the full.

The following year Alex proudly informed us that he was going to be a Dad, Emily was ecstatic beyond belief and I was as pleased as punch. Not to be outdone, a few weeks later Edward announced impending fatherhood. Emily was only slightly calmer this time around.

Everything went well, and our first grandson was born at Halloween, followed by our granddaughter on Christmas Eve. Unlike me in my youth, my sons were present for the happy events.

David set up home with Anne, and I was very happy about this, for I could see that she was good for him, and kept his feet firmly on the ground. David was a party animal, but Anne knew how to rein him in, she was no soft touch, and was exactly what he needed. David now worked in a hotel and although the pay was not great, he seemed to be reasonably happy with his lot.

I injured my back at work and although it was not serious, it did curtail my ability to do the physical side of the job.

I had never been a manager who sat on his backside, and let others do the work. I could not justify more than about six hours of office duties in any week, and was becoming very bored with sitting around doing nothing. My boss told me to supervise and take it easy, but my staff needed very little guidance and would not appreciate me looking over their shoulder all day.

An opportunity arose for a new career selling fertiliser and chemicals to golf courses. I reckoned that if I kept trying to do the physical work I would probably be crippled before retirement. So I applied and off I went for my interview for this new position.

I left an hour before I needed to but still managed to be late. A lorry had shed its load, and the police were diverting all traffic. I followed the diversion signs only to end up at the back of the queue we had just left. It could only happen in Ireland was the thought that sprang to mind as I phoned ahead and made my apologies.

I was given the job and this would mean big changes in our lives. I would have to buy a house, the tied cottage was no longer an option. At the sprightly age of forty nine I became a first time buyer.

Most normal people my age were coming to the end of their mortgage when I was starting mine. We bought cheap and a lot of DIY was needed to make the house habitable, but my old boss gave me six months grace to vacate the house, for we had improved his property while we were there, and I had waited six months to get it in the first place.

No more driving old bangers, a company car was included in the deal. The new boss did not give any sales target, he just said go out and see how you get on. After a couple of months I insisted on knowing what they expected. The boss told me £300,000 would be very satisfactory, but it would take me at least two years to reach this. I did over £400,000 in my first year and continued to increase sales until the recession hit.

Things are much tougher now but I still work in the same job. All things considered they have been very understanding about the downturn. They know I'm still out there getting what little business is available.

The Challenges of Life

One of my younger sisters had been ill for a long time with a rare lung disease, she needed a new lung, but none compatible had been found. Now bedridden and on oxygen, the prognosis was not good. If no suitable donor was found soon she would not survive, in her weakened condition it was doubtful if she could survive the operation, even if a lung was found.

She was still only in her early forties, with a loving husband, and two young sons. I thought to myself of all my siblings, she was the one who never abused her body, why couldn't it be me. Life doesn't always serve up happy endings, and we lost her soon afterwards.

The family rallied round and we got through the funeral as best we could, we were all devastated, but I think it hit my Dad more than most. I felt like a little lost boy and did what was asked of me, but I really wasn't much help to anyone, for I was frightened that I might drink over this. I had no desire to drink, but I wondered if this sort of trauma might prompt the return of the madness. I went to plenty of meetings over the next few weeks, and gradually my fear subsided.

I believe that the longevity of my sister's illness had given me time to mentally prepare for the tragic outcome, and this helped me to weather the storm.

Mum has often said that Dad was never the same after this tragedy, and it was not much more than a year later that he was taken ill. He had to go in for a hernia operation and he was delighted, for he had convinced himself that he had cancer. After the operation he was still very poorly, and was again taken in to hospital.

I was at a trade conference in Limerick when my brother phoned me very late one cold March night. He said I'd better get home, for Dad had taken a turn for the worse, and it did not look good. I wanted to run out the door, and drive home straight away, but I was in no fit state to drive 200 miles in the middle of the night. I had no drink taken, but I was extremely tired, and reasoned that my family might be attending my funeral if I left now.

I left very early next morning, and thankfully I made it back to see Dad before his passing. I was better able to cope with this death, and played my part in making the necessary arrangements for his funeral.

Not many people get over sixty years of happy marriage, and Dad had led a full, and active life before going in to hospital. This did not make his passing any less painful, but it did make it easier to accept. Thoughts of drink never entered my head during this time of grieving, nor did the fear of those thoughts.

I had completely accepted that I could not take alcohol, and had no interest in what it had to offer. My sobriety had become second nature in the same way that getting drunk had been second nature when I was younger. The "Good Wolf" within was in control.

Wedding bells were ringing once again, for Lisa and Richard had decided to get married, and the wedding was to be in Scotland. I asked her to consider coming home for the occasion, and was quickly told that Scotland was her home now. This was not said in a hurtful, or churlish way, but it made me realise that our kids no longer needed us in the way they did when they were young.

They were adults now with their own ideas, and were fiercely independent. They knew how to look after themselves, and were confident in their ability to run their own affairs.

This made me very proud not only of them, but of Emily, for the way she had raised them, through those early years, when I was a drunk.

I make no apologies for saying that Lisa's wedding was the most memorable for me. She is my only daughter, and as the father of the bride, I was much more closely involved with the wedding arrangements.

The setting for the marriage meant that we would have to go to Scotland to finalise arrangements for the day. The church was in a small village on the bonnie banks of Loch Lomond that had featured in a popular television series.

This fame made it one of the most popular wedding venues in Scotland, and much to my surprise, the church was rigged for live video streaming via the internet, my Mum, who was too frail to travel to the wedding, got to watch it live on my brother's computer.

Once again we had a wonderful day, with temperatures soaring above thirty degrees, the winter weight kilts were uncomfortable, but it didn't matter. At the reception we dined looking out over Loch Lomond, and I will never forget the happiness radiated by the Bride & Groom.

He must have loved Lisa very much, for he was missing England's opening match in the world cup finals to be there. (England won, and so did Richard)

It was also lovely to have our grandchildren there with us, including the latest addition to the clan. Marie had provided Alex with a beautiful baby daughter, just a few weeks before the wedding.

Our marriage was stronger than it had ever been, we rarely had cross words and were very happy. Seeing our kids grow up into decent, caring adults, in stable relationships and enjoying life, was worth more to me than a lottery win.

My fear that some of them might go through the madness I lived with in my early years was groundless. We were very proud, and had a good relationship with all of them.

Three weddings, and buying a house in less than six years, it was time for a proper holiday for us. We booked a Mediterranean cruise for a week the following summer. This would be our first ever foreign holiday, and we intended to make the most of it, but first we had Christmas to organise.

Christmas is a special time, and with the kids all grown up, and scattered around different parts of the country, it was difficult to find a way to bring us all together.

We decided to hold an annual Christmas lunch, a couple of weeks before the holiday. This has become a tradition with us, and is our Christmas present to them. Besides I hate wrapping presents, this is a much simpler arrangement, and something we look forward to every year. With the busy lives they all lead, it can be difficult to find a date to suit everybody, they all make it most years to this special family day.

Of course the grand kids are also invited, and another one of these arrived when Emma gave Edward a son not long after we returned from our cruise. They really know how to treat you well aboard ship, and seeing six cities, in three different countries was a great experience.

On our first night onboard we got friendly with a couple from Portrush who were old hands at cruising, they gave us some valuable tips on how to get the most from our voyage. We were in the cabaret bar when I noticed that our new friend was drinking coke just like me. I asked if he knew "Bill W" (one of the founders of A.A.) and he did.

What are the chances of becoming friendly with a total stranger on a foreign holiday, who is a member of the fellowship? Better than you might think, there are thousands of us getting on well in life without taking drink.

We had a great time, although I'm not a gambler I did try the casino just to see what it was like. I made enough in one night to put a third down as a deposit for next year's cruise, which we booked while still on board. At the end of the week we said goodbye to our new friends, who were staying aboard for another week, and headed home content in the knowledge that we would be back next year.

A few months later David and Anne told us they had set the date for their wedding. It was arranged for July 2009, nearly two years hence. We knew this was coming and were very happy for them. I was glad it was not sooner, for we were committed to our cruise next summer, and needed time to save for their big day. Life was good to us and soon we were off on our second cruise.

At the airport we got talking to a young couple who had been married the day before and had barely had time to change, before coming to the airport to go cruising on their honeymoon.

We wished them the best of luck, and I persuaded the cabin crew to announce their marriage with a champagne toast mid-flight.

This put an idea in my head, and after discussing it with Emily we again booked a cruise when we reached the ship. This time it was a wedding present for David and Anne. Our friends from last year were also in the queue, and it was good to see familiar faces. They say there are no coincidences in A.A. perhaps they're right.

We toured a cathedral in Valencia, and when the tour guide reverently told us we were looking at the "Holy Grail", I asked a whispered question to a tall blonde beside me. I said "Do you think Indiana Jones knows about this?"She took a fit of the giggles, the tour guide was not amused, and I got a punch in the arm from the tall blonde, and a dirty look from my wife.

Another great holiday, and it was off home to start making arrangements for David's wedding. I wanted to keep their wedding present a secret, but they might book something else so this was not practical. They were over the moon with the gift, and it was worth every penny, just to see their faces light up when we told them. This was to be slightly different from the other weddings.

The ceremony would be in the same hotel as the reception. The months rolled by quickly, and soon the big day arrived. Once again the day was a great success.

David had always been the quiet one of our kids, and everybody thought he would struggle with his speech. But he had prepared well, and did himself and his new wife proud, with the best speech from any of the weddings.

He finished it by presenting his bride with a ball & chain, much to the amusement of all present. They enjoyed their day to the full, and we partied late into the night.

A few days later they were off on their cruise, with a mid-flight champagne toast that I had managed to keep as a surprise for them.

I had a peace and contentment that I never believed possible, and could not wish for a better life. I continued to enjoy these gifts because although I no longer went to meetings, I still practiced the twelve step programme.

I had drifted away from A.A. meetings during the last few years, and rarely went nowadays. I was confident in my sobriety, and never had any thoughts about taking a drink.

I had not allowed myself to forget my last drunk, and was fully aware that if I did not live a decent life, and treat people properly, I could easily fall off the wagon. The "Bad Wolf" within had been dormant for several years, I knew he was still there, but I no longer feared him the way I once had.

Life presents us with many challenges, and the quality of my sobriety would soon be tested by a tragedy nobody expected. I received a phone call telling me that my oldest sister was in hospital. Her husband had been unable to rouse her from her sleep that morning, and had called an ambulance.

Never sick, always out in the garden she loved, the last of my siblings I would have worried about getting ill, was lying unconscious in a hospital bed. I was not far from the hospital, when I got there some of the family had already gathered, and I knew things were not good.

She had suffered a ruptured aneurysm, and never regained consciousness. This was different from previous bereavements. I was mentally prepared before, but not this time. The suddenness of her passing left me in total shock.

The sight of her husband and their children, in complete devastation broke my heart. I knew I had to hold myself together for the sake of the family, but anger was welling up within me. It was not fair to take one who radiated kindness and love so much, that she was loved by everyone who met her. I managed to control my emotions, and did my duty to the family, but I was falling apart inside.

On a cold November day, with snow lying all around, I looked at my Mum. She was sitting on a seat in the street behind the funeral car containing her first born child. She was in her eighties and looked cold and frail, but would not go inside until the hearse departed.

As her children gathered around, trying to shield her from the cold wind, she looked straight at me and said "will you be alright?" She never asked that question of any of my siblings. Over twenty years since my last drink, but she was still frightened that I might hit the bottle.

I bore no resentment from her words, for I knew she spoke only out of love for me. I smiled, and reassured her that I was fine. This was a lie, for my only thought was "what's the fucking point", my mind was in turmoil.

I had no thought of taking a drink, but I knew that if I couldn't shake off the negativity growing in me, sooner or later drink would become an option. The "Bad Wolf" within had awakened and was clawing at my throat. I was more vulnerable than I had been for many years, however I was not the soft touch I had been in my youth, and I knew what to do to keep him at bay.

After several years of absence I went back to A.A. The old thought that had helped me in the past came back. "Don't go back to the madness, you've too much to lose" I now had an army behind me, and shared what I was feeling. Slowly the gloom lifted, and the "Bad Wolf" within was once again locked in his cage. The urge to drink never returned, but I will continue to reinforce my sobriety by attending A.A. on a regular basis.

I enjoy my meetings, and hopefully I can pass on the gift I was so freely given by the members of A.A. It's been eighteen months since my sister's untimely death, and I still have not got the same peace of mind I had before she passed away.

Each day I grow stronger and positivity rules the roost once again. I hope these last couple of chapters have shown that there can be a good life after booze, no matter what life throw's at you.

The challenges I have overcome give me confidence in my ability to cope with whatever lies ahead. I know that I never have to drink again, provided I try to live the right way.

The principles of the twelve step programme show me how to live with peace in my head.

The world is a good place to be because I got honest with myself, changed my attitude, and learnt to live in the day, not in my fears.

Conclusion

There will be fifteen at Christmas lunch this year for we now have another grandson, any more and I'll need a second mortgage to pay the bill, but I'll gladly pay it to see my family together, for I know that I came close to losing them when I was a drunk.

I have been married to Emily for almost thirty six years, why she put up with me is still a mystery. I can't turn back the clock and right the wrongs of my drinking career. But I can make amends by staying sober, and adding to the lives of those close to me, instead of taking from them as I once did.

Once again I humbly thank all those members of A.A. who have helped me through the years, and hope I have also helped them in some way with my sharing. Most of all I thank my darling Emily, who suffered terribly through my drunken years, but never gave up on me. If she had, I don't think I'd be here today to write this.

As I finish my tale I ask one favour of you

Whether you be a drunk, teetotal, or anything in between. When life gets tough and things aren't going your way, when despair and negativity start to take control. Stop and think of my story, and the parable below, which I am led to believe is taken from ancient teachings.

A troubled student went to his mentor and said

"Master, I have bad thoughts in my head and they make me ashamed"

"I also have these thoughts my son, within each of us there is a good wolf and a bad wolf and they forever battle to control our minds"

"Master please tell me, which wolf will win the battle?"

"The one you feed the most my son"

The Question Is

WHICH WOLF WILL YOU FEED TODAY?

THE END

By a Grateful Alcoholic, known as: Davy E.

The Grateful Alcoholic

As a kid growing up I was always lonely
I'd join in sometimes but shyness owned me
Exams were easy I was not a fool
But I couldn't wait to get out of school

In my world of dreams I did what I wanted
In fantasy land my wishes were granted
As a superhero or a football star
I'd live my dreams and drive a big sports car

When I reached my teens I was a mixed up kid
It wasn't long before I hit the skids
Escaping into that golden bottle
I kept my foot hard down upon the throttle

I didn't know for it went unspoken
My parent's hearts were almost broken
In fear and anguish I tried to fix my life
I eased up on the booze and found a wife

It wasn't long before heavy drinking
Came back again what was I thinking!
God help that girl she'd an awful life
My drink brought nothing but fear and strife

With kids to feed she soldiered on
I didn't care I was too far was gone
In complete oblivion my heart got colder
My evil side grew ever bolder

I remember little of those terrible times
Alcoholic blackouts hid my shameful crimes
It's always darkest before the dawn
My conscience spoke this could not go on

I kick and screamed I fought the madness
I couldn't live this life of badness
I often thought that I couldn't win
My self esteem was in the bin

Alone I didn't stand a chance
The drink led me a merry dance
I needed help and in desperation
I found the path to my salvation

Ex drunks saved me in smoke filled rooms
There was hope that I could lift the gloom
I was not alone there were others like me
The drink was gone and I was set free

I learned to live a much better life
I found some peace for me and the wife
I've never returned to that awful booze
Life's far too good I've too much to lose

My only regret is I took too long
To see the light and right the wrongs
I still find it hard to show emotion
To those I love with complete devotion

So in these words I hope you'll find
An understanding of my crazy mind
For the pain I caused I'm very sorry
But you no longer need to worry

I live in today I don't fear tomorrow
I've peace in my head not hate and sorrow
Is there an afterlife? I have my doubts
When I pop my clogs I'll soon find out

If there is a heaven and a hell
It's down I'll go to ring Satan's bell
Behind my back I'll be holding something
He'll wonder what I'm hiding from him

The sheet of paper I've brought to show him
Is a copy of the twelve step programme
By the time He's read beyond step seven
He'll know I'm trouble and send me to Heaven

When I talk with God I'll seek his grace
To keep a smile on my family's face
I don't want my kids to mourn for me
I got a second chance and lived life free

I f my wife survives me and I hope she can
She'll be well looked after by the rest of the clan
I'll look down on them from the stars above
With a smile on my face and a heart full of love

I've made my peace and have no fear
So smile for me don't shed a tear
My friends will arrive and after our greetings
We'll be off to find an A.A. meeting.

By Davy E.

*The Twelve Step Programme

1 We admitted we were powerless over alcohol—that our lives had become unmanageable.

2 Came to believe that a Power greater than ourselves could restore us to sanity.

3 Made a decision to turn our will and our lives over to the care of God as we understood Him.

4 Made a searching and fearless moral inventory of ourselves.

5 Admitted to God, to ourselves, and to another human being the exact nature of our wrongs.

6 Were entirely ready to have God remove all these defects of character.

7 Humbly asked Him to remove our shortcomings.

8 Made a list of all persons we had harmed, and became willing to make amends to them all.

9 Made direct amends to such people wherever possible, except when to do so would injure them or others.

10 Continued to take personal inventory, and when we were wrong, promptly admitted it.

11 Sought through prayer and meditation to improve our conscious contact with God as we understood Him, praying only for knowledge of His will for us and the power to carry that out.

12 Having had a spiritual awakening as the result of these steps, we tried to carry this message to alcoholics, and to practice these principles in all our affairs.*

My thanks to "AAWS" for granting me permission to re-print the steps.

Davy E.

Printed by Amazon Italia Logistica S.r.l.
Torrazza Piemonte (TO), Italy

66101385R00103